PRAISE FOR

"This book is an example [...] a practical tool for personal and Spiritual transformation. It is a unique accomplishment, and takes a great deal of courage, ingenuity, faith and creative savvy to commit to paper-let alone outline the very methodology and tools after each chapter for achieving growth and freedom. Dawn's vision quest in the footsteps of the Unicorn's journey is a creative adventure story in itself. Going beyond the story and creating exercises and things to do to overcome internal blocks to personal Spiritual alignment - is a stroke of genius which turns the book into an accessible practical tool toward realizing inner self and balance. Simply, this book is a deep and meaningful spiritual contribution to the human journey."

—Pauline Sandell, Global Age Life Coach, Phoenix, AZ

"Dawn is a straight shooter with the Word of God. She's been an example of humility for me, ever yielded to the Holy Spirit. I credit her ministry and friendship for saving my life!"

—Cherie Marshall-Cooper, Founder/CEO Sweet Pie Desserts, Gilbert, AZ

"Dawn has been a life-line through my darkest times. Her prophetic words are rich with life giving health and encouragement for she is a conduit in which the Holy Spirit speaks. I highly recommend this book!"

—Madelyn Smith, Horn of Hope Ministries, Florida

"In my business, I love making women feel beautiful on the inside, and radiating that beauty with make-up and hair, accentuating those features on the outside. BUT! When Dawn left my salon, I felt like she did that for me. I felt so different after she left, like, that was a once in a lifetime person and I think SHE changed ME. A moment of divinity, Divine intervention, if you will. Her book will bless you!"

—Amanda Victoria, Amanda Victoria Beauty, 2017 Pick by The Knot, best of weddings Avondale, AZ

The UNICORN, the DONKEY and DARLING

First published by My Father's Pen December 2017

ISBN 13: 978-0-9997097-0-2

The Unicorn, the Donkey and Darling Copyright ©2017 by Dawn Lindsay

All rights reserved. No part of this publication may be reproduced, stored in a retrieval system, or transmitted in any form or by any means, to include electronic, mechanical, photocopying, recording, or otherwise, without the prior written permission of the author.

All scripture quotations are taken from the KING JAMES VERSION (KJV) unless marked otherwise. KING JAMES VERSION, public domain.

Scriptures marked NAS are taken from the NEW AMERICAN STANDARD (NAS): Scripture taken from the NEW AMERICAN STANDARD BIBLE®, copyright© 1960, 1962, 1963, 1968, 1971, 1972, 1975, 1977, 1995 by The Lockman Foundation. Used by permission.

Scriptures marked NIV are taken from the NEW INTERNATIONAL VERSION (NIV): Scripture taken from THE HOLY BIBLE, NEW INTERNATIONAL VERSION®. Copyright© 1973, 1978, 1984, 2011 by Biblica, Inc.™. Used by permission of Zondervan. Scriptures marked NKJV are taken from the NEW KING JAMES VERSION (NKJV): Scripture taken from the NEW KING JAMES VERSION®. Copyright© 1982 by Thomas Nelson, Inc. Used by permission. All rights reserved.

Scriptures marked NSECB are taken from the NEW STRONG'S EXHAUSTIVE CONCORDANCE OF THE BIBLE: All Greek and Hebrew words are italicized. They are taken from the NEW STRONG'S EXHAUSTIVE CONCORDANCE OF THE BIBLE, James Strong, 1990 copyright© by Thomas Nelson Publishers.

Book design by Adam Robinson for Good Book Developers.

Author photo by Walter Larsen Images, www.wlimages.com

Printed in the United States of America.

The UNICORN, the DONKEY and DARLING

Journey from Dissociation to Integration

by Dawn Lindsay

Contents

A Note from the Author	*xi*
Never Mind Trail	*1*
The First Wall	4
We Like Sheep Have Gone Our Own Way	
The Second & Third Walls	12
People and a Broken Heart	
The Fourth Wall	18
Little Fences	
The Fifth Wall	29
A Fortress of Accusations	
The Sixth Wall	37
Hope Deferred	
The Seventh Wall	57
Intimidation	
The Eighth Wall	72
A Very Small Box	
The Ninth & Tenth Walls	79
Others and an Ancient Key	

The Eleventh Wall	90
A Crowd on a Foggy Day	
The Twelfth Wall	100
The Loss of Ground & an Unlikely Teacher	
The Thirteenth Wall	125
Isolated in Fragmented Memories	
The Fourteenth Wall	141
Skin Is a Veil	
Glossary	*151*
Resources for Deeper Study	*167*
Meet the Author	*168*
Acknowledgements	*170*
Workshops	*174*

This book is dedicated to my mother,
Barbara Darlene Taylor,
who saw more in me than I saw in myself. The visionary seeds you sowed into my life took root and have blossomed into this parable! Your unyielding dedication to your children, honest encouragement and love are an eternal imprint upon my heart. You poured your love, laughter, wisdom and time into my life, and I cherish those memories we made together. There couldn't have been a better mother for me. Thank-you, Jesus, for giving her to me!

A Note from the Author

THIS BOOK CAME TO ME IN A CONTINUING vision occurring each time I entered into my prayer time with the Lover of my soul, Jesus Christ. Along with the vision came the word "integrate." It is a simplistic parable of the integration of The Unicorn, symbolizing the Holy Spirit, the Donkey, symbolizing the body, and Darling, symbolizing the soul. Darling is our lead character, narrating her journey to wholeness. Her name is taken from Ps. 22, the foreshadowing of Messiah's crucifixion, during which He refers to His soul as "my darling."

The story takes us on a journey to wholeness, through dissociation to integration. Dissociation is the plight of mankind. We have forgotten where we came from, who we are, who our Father is, and why we are here. This, I call dissociation. It is a term meaning to be out of association. In the case of God's people, we desire to be in association with

Him, the Lover of our soul. The only way is through Jesus Christ, the Way, the Truth and the Life. We are to follow His example in order to return to fellowship, association, with our Father.

It has since been said that such conditions of brokenness are not healed through therapy, but one is taught how to manage through life in spite of such dissociation. It is my personal testimony that while therapy certainly does help, healing only comes through Jesus Christ, Yeshua ha Meshiach, our Savior, Redeemer, Deliverer, the One God, who is Whole - Spirit, Soul and Body. We are to be holy as He is Holy, through Grace alone, His Righteousness, of course. Not our own. And this holiness, I am convinced, centers around being One with Him, integrated, not dissociated.

Webster's New Twentieth Century Second Edition, 1935 Dictionary defines integrate as, "to make whole, renew or complete by adding or bringing together parts." This is the focus of our story. The renewing of the mind is a continual process, "until Christ be formed in you," (Gal. 4:19), not just His character, but His mind, a sound mind, undivided. "A double-minded man is unstable in all his ways," (James 1:8). Double-minded means to be "two spirited," (Strongs #1374) "vacillating between two opinions or purposes: (**Double-minded**"), which brings us right back to holiness. This can only come by His grace, of course, as we "walk out our salvation with fear and trembling" (Phil. 2:12).

Dissociation is a splintered or fractured state of being. It's what we do when the current situation is more than we can bear. So, instead of retreating into the Spirit of God, we retreat into an "other" spirit or reality or fantasy; an idol, really. This is a method of survival for people in traumatic situations, real or perceived and is allowed by the Lord until the soul is ready to be healed.

Unicorn is used in the story to symbolize the Spirit of God dwelling in the spirit of man, secret place (the Garden), the Holy of Holies within the believer. It is that place where the soul longs to return to the full-time communion with its Creator.

The King James Version is the only version of the Bible that I've found "wild ox" translated as "unicorn" (Strong's #7214, a wild bull [from its conspicuousness] from #7213, *ra'am,* meaning to rise: -be lifted up). Unicorn, or its plural form, unicorns, is used nine times in the King James Version. Since the vision given to me contained a unicorn to depict the Holy Spirit within me, I chose to be true to the vision given.

In folklore, the unicorn is said to be a powerful, one of a kind, pure and mystical creature, who only reveals itself to a pure virgin, with whom it can be at peace, resting its' head upon her lap. It is a picture of the Holy Spirit who is untamable, an overcoming warrior, whose horn symbolizes power and authority (Ps. 132:17,18) and is connected to King David's crown.

Donkey represents the body. The body never lies. Our soul may be sleeping, but the body functions continuously at a more primal level, or else our heart would stop beating and our lungs would stop breathing.

Walls refer to a mindset or idol, which isolates, separates the soul from hearing the voice of God and communing with Him. They also hinder us from doing the will of God. In this book, they symbolize the dissociation tool of the mind.

Most of us are fragmented to some degree or another depending upon personal traumas and the particular call upon the individual life. It is a universal struggle, then, to remember who we are, where we came from and why we are here.

Regarding these things, we all have memory loss to some degree. And to some degree, we have all given our "land" over to interlopers and walled ourselves into small places.

My hope is that this little book will help you remember who you are, how precious you are, and that you are loved beyond deserving. May you fully integrate the pieces of your true essence from all of the "lands" to which you have dispersed your true soul, your darling. May you truly know Him in the fullness of your whole self, being transformed into the very likeness of Him.

Sincerely and in His Love,

Dawn

Never Mind Trail

"The carnal mind is enmity against the Lord"

Rom. 8:7

WALKING ALONGSIDE A NEW TRAIL, I NOTICED two trees standing in the lush garden of our land. Rather, two tree-bushes, I suppose. It's hard to tell! Short in stature, about the height of a tall man, but added girth. They were completely leafless and bore long, thorn-like branches. Among the desert green branches were dry branches shamefully displaying their lifeless dull brown of death.

Walking toward them, love swept over me bringing affection for the first tree. I was pained at the burden the tree-bush felt, having to support the heaviness of death hanging in the branches but still attached to the trunk.

Moved by compassion, I broke off as many branches of death as possible. Then I kicked with all my might at those remaining until my strength had proven to be insufficient to finish the job without tools. Stepping back, satisfaction filled my soul, as the tree-bush had begun to look more like a tree. But knowing I could do no more without tools, I turned, took three steps away and heard a voice behind me say, "Thank-you!" Spinning around, I saw only the tree! I laughed spontaneously with all that was within me. The tree impressed its gratitude into my soul, expressing its relief from the drain of dead branches. The strength and energy required to bear the weight of dead branches consumed all available resources to grow tall, thus stunting the trees' stature.

Looking aside to the trail, but still smiling from this unusual encounter, I began to concern myself that anyone walking along the trail who might see me would think I was crazy, talking to a tree! Then it came to me, Talking Tree! What a perfect name, an appropriate name for this half-transformed tree-bush.

Looking back at Talking Tree, the conversation continued. "I am of the species, Crucifixion Thorn. I was used as a crown for the Saviors crucifixion. It was fashioned into a crown because the carnal mind is enmity against the Lord. The mind and all of its beliefs, lies and self-deluding thoughts, self-sufficiency, second-guessing and rationalizing the Still Small Voice, all usurping the authority of God within His own temple. They are dead branches that must be pruned, just like me, Talking Tree. This is the beginning of the process, walking through life on the nearby trail. Spirit-led life is the goal. Our Creator said, "…as many as are led by the Spirit of God, they are the sons of God." Wholeness comes at a cost, your self-sufficiency dependence on your own strategies instead of dependence on the Holy Spirit of God within you."

> *5 "Trust in the Lord with all your heart*
> *lean not on your own understanding.*
> *6 In all of your ways acknowledge Him*
> *and He shall direct thy paths."*
> *Prov. 3:5,6*

I lay the trail before you, Darling. Follow it and see where it leads. The only pain is that of postponement."

Looking beyond Talking Tree, the trail came into focus and I was compelled to follow it wherever it led. A sign on the edge of the narrow path introduced me to Never Mind Trail.

(ROMANS 8:7, 8:14; PROV. 3:5,6)

The First Wall

We Like Sheep Have Gone Our Own Way

During a particularly difficult and confusing time of life, I spied a unicorn in my garden eating of the fruit therein. Brilliant white coat, long, feathery mane and tail softly dancing in the wind. It is well known that a unicorn is untamable and could be quite dangerous. His presence, however, radiated peace and power, compassion and a gentleness of spirit, which enticed my heart to get closer. Strong- jawed like a horse, regal, confident, but at the same time his essence felt safe, almost childlike, but with a power and authority unparalleled. Flashing blue eyes peeked from behind the curtain of his mane, revealing a surprisingly shy and respectful nature. One impressive horn spiraled from his forehead silently demanding respect from all who catch a glimpse of him.

While gazing upon his beauty, I heard the Holy

Spirit say to me, "Darling, there are fourteen walls to overcome within your soul. All deter the continuation on Never Mind Trail causing unnecessary pain and suffering; suffering due to the distractions of these walls within your soul. Your focus departs from Me and centers upon the circumstances of the past, present or future days. With the elimination of each wall, you are afforded a little more space within your very essence to extend both spiritual and physical borders of your life. "Enlarge the place of your tent!" the prophet declared. This is that. You become more yourself the one you abandoned, with each wall that is overcome. The shattered pieces of your self are coming together in one accord. You have been disjointed in spirit, soul and body making it difficult to be consistent in your life. You, Darling, can see this journey on Never Mind Trail as the integration of your whole self being unified in Me. Each wall is more deeply seated within you, thereby revealing the great robbery each has stolen from your joy. They must all be released for you to live in the freedom and fullness I desire for you. These fourteen walls in your thinking will be torn down, not jumped. One of the purposes of a wall is to test your resolve. In other words, to test how badly you want something, namely, Me. The job will be done with ease. And," Spirit said, "we can do it all now."

Struck with awe, I watched as he approached a red brick wall only three rows high. He could have jumped it easily, but instead he touched it with his single, spiral horn. As fast as you can snap your fingers, the wall crumbled down to the ground. And I wept. For this wall represented a business failure, something I ought not to have embarked upon since Spirit had said not to do it in the first place. Our rebellions bring shame and can lead us into the spirit of the world and out of His abiding peace. This is precisely what happened. And I paid bitterly for it, in loss of peace and reputation. But after the demise of this wall, I felt no shame.

The debris he simply stepped over.

(Isaiah 53:6; 54:2 NAS)

Between the Walls

God's Bubble

"My grace is sufficient for thee; for my strength is made perfect in weakness"

2 COR. 12:9

BETWEEN THE WALLS IS LIKE BEING SUSPENDED between heaven and earth, God's bubble as I call it. The workings of the Divine Therapist are sometimes in the ordinary events of life, the comings and goings of family, friends and business within the regular stuff everyday. At other times, interventions of a noticeably supernatural nature occur within the four elements of this realm, yet time and this material world seem distant. While being bodily held within earth's realm the soul sees with spiritual eyes, hears with spiritual ears the beauty, wisdom and wonder of the Maker of Heaven and Earth. While caught-up in the heavenly realm, under Loves' anesthesia, the Divine scalpel repairs the soul's fractures, healing emotions, traumas, and fears of all kinds. An awakening occurs and Darling, the soul, is deepened in knowledge, wisdom, but mostly love for the One Who Knows all.

The anesthesia of the Divine Therapist's working in the heart will wear off in a matter of hours, days or weeks, but the intoxicating Presence of Love Himself abides deeper and more profound with each caress of His all-seeing gaze. To be seen of Him, every crack, crevice and cave of your nature, and yet feel His love is like fresh oil upon your parched soul. For as long as you abide in the knowing of His Presence you are suspended above all stress and worry of this world, yet still within the world. Infused within your being are the lessons learned, wisdom gained from these interludes with the Lover of your soul. This soaking time enhances the souls' ability to remain in each healing.

Between the walls is where revelation comes to the soul. After a session with the Divine Therapist, a deeper peace comes forth and the soul finds rest with Him. While resting in His presence various degrees of understanding is infused into the soul. Learning without effort.

Your entire being longs to remain enveloped in Him, though you must follow Him wherever He leads, when He leads. If He leads you to the marketplace, you must go It's about obedience. When you know to do something and don't do it, it is sin. Sin is anything that separates you from abiding with God. It takes you into a different spirit. We are to acknowledge Him in everything we do and experience and think. When we fail, "He is faithful and just to forgive us our sins:" Each time we are disobedient, the more quickly we repent, the more quickly we are restored into a peaceful abiding with Him. It happens in seconds! Be quick to repent and come back into His loving Spirit.

It's all by His grace. We must continually be mindful that we are standing in His righteousness at all times. Otherwise, Holy God could not abide in the presence of unholiness. We would be burned up because his holiness is a consuming fire. Because of His outrageous love for us, he can abide in us; we can abide in Him because of the Blood He shed on the cross for our unholiness. Because of the blood transfusion we received when we accepted Him as our God, we are righteous at all times, no matter what condition our heart is in at the moment! His grace is like a big glass of orange juice is to our immune system. Come boldly to Him in these sessions between the walls and get your healing! He is willing and able to heal all of your pain, sorrow and brokenness.

I recommend that you begin to read the book of John again. It is full of the Father's love for you. Make it personal as you read it and if you haven't asked Him to be your God, to live in your heart and make you whole, let's do it now with this simple prayer:

> *Father, I am a faulty person. I have made many mistakes in this life and I am desiring to be made whole. I believe that you love me and want me. So please, come into my heart now, be my Lord and Savior. I want you, too! In Jesus name, Amen*

In our story, Darling knew that she wasn't supposed to embark upon that business venture, since the Holy Spirit had told her not to. He knew it wasn't going to turn out well for her, but she did it anyway. Jesus said, "If you love me, keep my commandments." It is good to notice that loving Him is directly related to doing what He says. Let yourself be humbled by the knowledge that you don't love Him as deeply as He deserves.

> *Father, Forgive me! I see that I am desperately failing in loving You, the One whom you gave your life for. I know that You alone are love, but I want to love You more! Please fill me with Your love! Thank-you, Father!*

(2 Cor. 12:9; 1John 1:9)

The Second & Third Walls

People and a Broken Heart

THE SECOND WALL WAS ALSO MADE OF RED brick, beautiful as it stood upon the complimentary green, tightly groomed grass crossing Never Mind trail. Again, the Unicorn simply and effortlessly, touched the wall. And with a certain gentleness and beauty the wall melted in obedience. I have never seen such a thing! As it melted a multitude of pastel colors emerged out of the red. They melted together like an impressionistic painting made of individual "bricks" of watercolor perfection. And I wept, for I loved this one very, very much. My tears, however, ceased abruptly when I realized that her prosperity would come much more quickly, now, for I had been holding her back with my fear. She so gracefully laid, now, like warm wax across the green pasture, ready to flow in life with peace.

Connected to her and in her shadow was what had been an identical but smaller red brick wall. When the first and larger wall turned to warm wax, this smaller one turned into ceramic baby blocks of blue, yellow, pink and green. The alphabets, ABC to Z were randomly placed within this wall's design.

As I watched, the blocks laid themselves in a single line upon the warm wax, as if to say, "This is my mother. I am bonded to her and I am her responsibility." I wept for the release of my false responsibility and then for the beauty of the rightness of it all.

The unicorn paused and looked at the sight of mother and child with reverent delight. His love for the two was immense. So much so, I could feel his heart tugging because he didn't want to walk away. Deeply I wept with a broken heart. The unicorn lingered there for a long time, just watching the two. While they were engrossed in each other, the unicorn backed away unnoticed.

With head held high, he traveled on. I marveled at this, since *my* heart still hurting.

Softly, understanding grew as a sunrise over the horizon. Sometimes my grief must be carried away for the benefit of others. That's why his head is held so high, because his heart is so low. His eyes are fixed upon the Lover of his soul.

As he walked on I could see the manifestation of his heart on the outside, as if there were no flesh and fur to contain it. I marveled at this sight, for his heart was red-orange with yellow and in the shape of a heart. Radiant heat and beams of light permeated his whole chest and extending way beyond his physical form. This was the effect of love's work, which revealed the truth and understanding about appropriate boundaries. He had to get out of the way so the new generation could come forth in power, like butterflies from the cocoon.

Although the unicorn had much power prior to this, he now exuded much more with the attribute of true love and obedience, which only comes through suffering.

Once finding the grace to know that suffering isn't always a result of being bad or of being a disappointment to others, truth can rise from the depths of pain, empowering the heart with freedom to be and move through life. "In Him we live and move and have our being."

(ACTS 17:28)

Between the Walls

False Responsibilities

So many ways a soul can suffer broken-heartedness; so many situations can cause a heart to break. Think of one time your heart was broken. Allow yourself to feel the pain this last time. Cry for as long and as hard as you need to. In your imagination, see yourself give all of your pain, sorrow and grief to Jesus. Now, choose to forgive the person who broke your heart and cancel the debt as in Mat. 6:9-15. Cast out the spirits of pain and trauma, in Jesus' name. Close the door to pain and trauma and seal it with the Blood of Jesus Christ. Leaving Egypt was scary for God's people. But they sealed their houses with the Blood of the Lamb over their doors. See the historical account in Exodus.

In like manner, we as believers in Yeshua, Jesus Christ, can apply the Blood of Jesus upon ourselves as we are being delivered out of slavery. We, the children of God, have been given all power and authority over sickness and demons. See Luke 9:1,2.

Regarding false responsibilities, we are only called to love others as we love ourselves. Many believe that this scripture is telling us to save others by rescuing them from suffering the consequences of their choices in life. Instead, we may be paying the price for their sins and preventing the Holy Spirit from teaching them the things they need to learn. It is sin to intervene this way and is an act of the flesh. The compassion of man gets in the way of God's pure compassion, and thwarts the working of God's righteousness. Instead, we are in God's way. Tell God you're sorry for preventing His will to be done in someone else's life and then get out of His way by trusting God with your loved ones. They will be blessed when you release your false responsibility. Life is much happier when we let God do what He's good at, and that is, transforming lives!

So, say,

Father, I repent for getting in Your way. I want to do Your will and I want to see my loved ones transformed. So, I release them into Your loving care. I know You love them much more than I do and I trust You to be their Savior. I am not their savior. I bless them, Father, and I thank-you for loving me even when I sin. So I let go of my guilt, which You paid for on the cross, in Jesus' name, Amen.

(MAT. 6:9-15; LUKE 9:1,2)

The Fourth Wall

Little Fences

WITH THIS NEWLY FOUND STRENGTH, Unicorn moved on to an even taller wall. I wondered how on earth he would overcome this one, since the last two had taken so long to recover from having broken his heart. I was tempted to stop the journey.

As Unicorn walked toward the next and higher wall, a wooden split rail fence extended across his path. He simply jumped over it, purposely looking back over his shoulder staring squarely into my eyes. He did this to remind me of the thoroughbred horse He had once used to teach me about myself.

The thoroughbred was powerful and fast, but his days of racing were now behind him. Having aged to the next phase of life, he began his jumping career. Once courageous and fearless, this horse had overcome many obstacles and won prestigious awards, ribbons and the accolades of many. He was well able in body, and remembered the days of adventurous success. But his mind was now fraught with fear from one single event.

It happened one day in autumn, while running through the pasture. The sun glistened across the pasture grass. A breeze shuffled the autumn colored leaves. He saw a sparkling in the distance. There, next to the old oak, stood a section of fence, and like a lightening bolt, ancient instinct by-passed his mind. Adrenaline shot through his body. Muscle memory pressed him on to perform his destiny one more time. He was made for this. His stride was set with perfect timing and geometry he subconsciously calculated. So focused upon the jump, and accustomed to flawless jumping arenas, he charged forward with a single vision of the fence. A flash of red broke his line of vision. A startled fox bounded across the grass breaking his concentration and his stride. Too late to recover from the distraction of the fox, his footing was off and he jumped too late. Graceful, long legs dragged across the barbed wire edge, dashing his flesh to the bone in some places. His heart now laced with fear, gave way to fearful caution, vowing never to jump again. "But I thought He made me for this!" Thus, he let that fox and that fence rob him of venturing beyond little fences into his destiny. It will keep him stuck and unable to move into his destiny, his passion in this life. Destiny awaits a horse that won't jump. Sometimes a wounded horse has to return to the beginning and start all over again.

To begin again with elementary principles the mind is retrained to live without fearful expectations. To begin again forms confidence in the heart and deepens the knowledge and understanding that formed the first foundation.

Remembering this story, understanding was infused into my mind. And I knew that nothing could hurt the Unicorn and keep him from *his* destiny. So I broke my vow to never try again. I reminded myself of how wonderful is the Lover of my soul!

Having left the little fence behind, Unicorn continued toward the next wall. He stopped in front of the wall, sat down and looked up at what I thought was the top of the wall, perhaps to measure its height. But, no, His sight extended to the heavenlies. He was seeking wisdom from the One who knows, the heavenly Father. He sat for a good long while, just listening. For he knew he must proceed with cautious precision, lest the wall fall upon him, crushing him.

As he sat, the courageous heart that had disappeared from my sight reappeared slowly. And his chest began to swell with a slight reddish tint to his white coat. If he could only hear his Father's command, he would charge ahead. But this was to be a delicate work produced by faith. And so, he trembled inside for respectful concern of destroying what was Holy. He was referring to the Donkey that followed him everywhere he went; for the body is holy, the temple of the Living God. A promise had been made centuries ago, a promise to be fulfilled at the end of the age.

With cautious precision, Unicorn stepped closer to the wall and pressed the point of his perfect horn against the wall. In an instant, without labor, a hole was formed. Once vacated, a small trickle of water emerged. And he instantly knew he must make another hole and another. With the third hole, a rumbling like an earthquake began growing in intensity and caused the mortar to crack.

Upon seeing this escalation of impending catastrophe, the unicorn simply stepped back. I was surprised for I had expected him to at least move aside. But no! He simply stepped back.

With a tumultuous sound, a flood came forth out of the side of the mountain. I thought for a moment that he did not prepare himself for the flood, or brace himself for falling rock. I questioned the wisdom of his decision and I trembled with fear. Surely the unicorn would drown, and us with him.

Instead, he was miraculously buoyed up with such great peace and floated *upstream*! The wall had been a dam, preventing God's prosperity of all blessings to flow. Because there is no loss in God, it was only stopped up. He always preserves until we are able to be buoyed up by our blessings rather than drown in misdirected affection for them. All affection for blessings must be given to the Giver of all.

Effortlessly he floated up-stream to the mouth of the deluge, where once again the jagged, rocky mountain was exposed.

This episode of rushing, water-like blessings filled the unicorn with mysterious buoyancy, even on dry land. He could now jump and leap great distances. He traveled so quickly, that I feared being left behind. Sensing this, he turned and looked back at me. His eyes flashed with a significance I had never seen before. He knew where he was going! He was focused. He was determined and fully persuaded of his calling. His jaw was set and the Donkey's chest expanded with purpose.

Suddenly I knew I could make it, too. For a moment, I felt a surge of confidence, as if Unicorn's sense of direction had become mine. I had always wanted to know where I was going in life, what my call was, always feeling a faint drawing toward a certain direction. However, the pull from within could be redirected by outside influences and circumstances. Somehow I felt impaired, as if it were a basic flaw in my genetic design. Not just flawed, deeply flawed. I wondered if I could ever get it right in life. Chin to the chest, eyes to the ground. My vision was earthbound again. Shame began to seep in through these thoughts where just a moment before significance and purpose had filled me through the Unicorns flashing eyes. A gap seemed to exist between us. I could not remain in that confident peace for more than minutes. Desperate, I lifted my eyes to grab another glimpse of his, hoping to regain what I had lost. When I did, curiosity replaced my shame. For Unicorn had morphed into the appearance of a donkey! I knew he was still the unicorn, because his essence could still be felt, that essence of peace, but his humble appearance was that of a gray, ordinary, sure-footed beast of burden. Were my eyes deceiving me? I wrestled with my thoughts. A sudden revelation struck me and I understood that I could sit upon his back at anytime that my strength waned. My eyes welled with tears since he seemed to know my needs without my saying so. I loved him all the more. His love for me made me able to do as he did. So I followed him. I wanted to be exactly what he wanted me to be, with him.

Between the Walls

Destiny Awaits

IN YOUR OWN LIFE, WHAT "LITTLE FENCES" HAVE you run into which caused you to stop running your race, jumping your hurdles? Ask Holy Spirit to bring them to mind and break any inner vows you created which are contrary to His destiny for you. A simple prayer like the following is perfect if you mean it. It's your kavenaugh, the intention of the heart that matters, not so much the exact words.

> *Father, You know my heart. If there be a little fence in my life that is keeping me from running to my destiny, please bring it to my understanding. If I made an ungodly vow I choose to break it now, in Jesus' name. I ask you to remove all consequences of those inner vows and forgive me of this sin. Have your way in me. Make me whole. Amen.*

Understanding is useful for the enlargement of
the soul as commanded in Isaiah 54:2-6 (NAS)

"Enlarge the place of your tent!"
Stretch out the curtains of your dwellings, spare not;
Lengthen your cords and strengthen your pegs.

For you will spread abroad to the right and to the left;
and your descendants (seed)
will possess nations,
And they will resettle the desolate cities.

Fear not, for you will not be put to shame:
Neither feel humiliated,
for you will not be disgraced;
But you will forget the shame of your youth,
And the reproach of your widowhood you will
remember no more
For your husband is your Maker,
Whose name is the Lord of hosts;
And your Redeemer is the Holy One of Israel.
Who is called the God of all the earth.

For the Lord has called you
Like a wife forsaken and grieved in spirit,
Even like a wife of one's youth
when she is rejected," Says your God.

Highlight the words that stand out to you. Now close your eyes and meditate upon those words. Write what comes to mind and highlight the main thread of continuity in your writing. What stands out? Have you ever felt like a desolate city? Write what that feels like. Was your youth filled with shame and humiliation?

Shame is a feeling that you are innately flawed; not that you did something wrong, but that you are something wrong. When shame overshadows a person, it diminishes the will of the soul to continue on God's given purpose and call, causing it to be self-focused on your own failings and not focused upon Him and His Truth about who He created you to be. All failures are recounted time and again making the soul doubt that God can use him/her at all. Thus the soul is paralyzed in it's own path. It loses its vision and becomes directionless.

To remedy this lie of shame, one needs only to renounce it in Jesus' name and begin to confess the truth over yourself, the truth of His Word. Ps. 139 is a beautiful place to start remembering who you are.

If married, has your husband rejected you; are you grieved in spirit, crushed, broken-hearted?

Did you ever consider that your husband is your Maker, your Redeemer, God of all the earth?

Deut. 23:23 says that a husband can veto a vow that his wife made! Your husband is Jesus, Yeshua! In His name you can break ungodly vows you have made. Confess your vows, repent and break them in Jesus' name. Let the Holy Spirit minister to you as He wishes.

(Is. 54:2-6; Ps.139: Deut. 23:23)

The Fifth Wall

A Fortress of Accusations

WITH THESE NEW REVELATIONS, THE FORtress up ahead began to shatter and fall down around us. Boulders of taunting words in the form of serpents mocked me with tails of shouting debris, which brought insecurity and emblazoned my emotions with doubt. I even began to doubt His love. I was empowered to know that the stones and boulders being lobbed toward us grew in force with the gravity of my gaze. Weighty words, words that burst through the air gained power over me if I paid attention to them, but looking past them the heavenly view became clear. Nothing could shatter us because nothing could hit us as long as I looked heavenward to see the Holy One's Word. So I lifted my eyes from the watching of my steps. It was then that I noticed the Donkey had been looking up the entire time. He knew how to trust. He knew his identity came from the Lord, not from the words of others. Desiring this strength of heart, I looked up to find his focus. I realized that we were approaching the place of the fort-like wall, rather, where it had been. For the stones were gone. As we passed, I began to feel confused, tired and weak. Grief came over me and I began to cry, but not knowing why. Donkey's back began to ache and I noticed random spots of swelling on his back. Inwardly perplexed, I pondered the oddity of the sudden onslaught of emotional distress and Donkey's bodily distress.

Then wisdom came to me. "Words spoken in secret and behind the back are as poisonous and deadly as words spoken to the face. Secret words are like a snake's fiery venom festering beneath the surface, swelling at the sight of entrance and quickly poisoning the entire body and soul." Infused knowledge from above came as I sought for the Unicorn's help. "Words can form a curse or a blessing. Unloving words inflict pain and depression and even create life or death. Speak life. Remove the cursed words and their effects, just like you would remove a knife. Then heal the wounds, physical, emotional and spiritual with words of life."

So I spoke over Donkey, "I remove the cursed

words and all of their effects from you. I forgive those who spoke them and I speak life to you, in Jesus name!"

Immediately the swollen spots disappeared and my tears ceased. Clarity of mind came along with joyful laughter!

And, I knew this was a necessary strengthening of my emotional heart. Words and accusations would no longer devastate and destroy my Darling, neither from within or without for my sight was aligned with the Donkey, heavenward, as we acknowledged Him.

Turning, now, to see where we had been and to breathe the fresh mountain air, I was pleased to recount the journey, thus far. So, I sat down at the right hip of the donkey and dangled my feet over the ledge of the newly conquered land. I began to write down all that had happened.

As I wrote, I leaned against his hip and found more and more inspiration. The donkey, meanwhile, drank water from three ancient wooden buckets, which had been prepared for us. Funny how *he* drank the water and *I* was refreshed! This inspiration was one benefit of overcoming the fort-like wall. Accusations from within and without had ceased. My attention was no longer redirected resulting in a siphoning-off of my physical energy.

As I wrote, leaning upon the donkey's hip, I realized that I was gaining strength and blessings with ability, merging as it were, with his strength. And I loved him all the more. He had stood still in the midst of falling stones so I could catch up with him.

And now, He stands and drinks while I am inspired and strengthened by him. The Unicorn who is so magnificently beautiful, pure white and one of a kind has made Himself my ordinary servant in the form of a humble Donkey.

(Prov. 18:21; Neh. 8:10)

Between the Walls

Serpents, Curses and Adder's Eggs

HARSH OR UNLOVING WORDS CAN STOP US ON our path. Genesis 49:17 says that "Dan shall be a serpent by the way, an adder in the *path* that bites the horses heels so that his rider shall *fall* backward." (Authors' emphasis) And that is the purpose of unloving words, to cause one to fall, as in the Garden of Eden. The serpent made his first appearance in Eden and caused mankind to fall. Serpents are symbolic of evil words, causing one to doubt Truth, Himself.

Speaking of evil men, Psalm 140:3 says, "They have sharpened their tongues like a serpent; adders' poison is under their lips. Selah." and Psalm 58:3,4 "...they go astray as soon as they are born, speaking lies. Their poison is like the poison of a serpent..." Dake's bible states, "When a slanderer speaks he conveys poison into the wound, as the serpent does. No reputation is safe before him, and against such there is little defense."

Adder in Strong's concordance is a kind of serpent (as snapping); from a root word meaning to overwhelm: break, bruise, and cover. Applied to your own words about yourself and others, the Lord has this to say, Prov. 6:2 "You are snared by the words of your mouth." When we speak, since our words have great power, we create much of our circumstances in this world. "Death and life are in the power of the tongue: and they that love it shall eat the fruit thereof" (Prov. 18:21) and God commands, "Speak life." Prov. 21:23 gives us a key to security. "Whoso keeps his mouth and his tongue keeps his soul from troubles."

What words have you spoken about others? What have you said regarding your life circumstances? What have you spoken about yourself, your health, your mind, and your time?

Isaiah 6:5 says," Woe is me! for I am undone; because I am a man of un lean lips, and I dwell in the midst of a people of unclean lips; for mine eyes have seen the King, the Lord of hosts." When we "see" the Lord in our revelation of His word, conviction strikes our soul. Ask the Lord to cleanse your lips and purify your heart, from which our words originate.

If your heart condemns you, then pray Isaiah 6:5. Ask our Father to help you clean up your heart because "A good man out of the good treasure of his heart brings forth good; and an evil man out of the evil treasure of his heart brings forth evil. For out of the abundance of the heart his mouth speaks." Luke 6:45 (NKJ)

If you desire good in your life then pray:

Father in heaven, my heart condemns me! I can see the fruit of my words in my life circumstances and relationships. I pray for Your forgiveness and I ask for a quick correction whenever I speak or am going to speak negative words about myself or others. Oh, please, Father, teach me your ways. "I want to know you and the power of your resurrection and the fellowship of your sufferings, being conformed to your death."(Phil. 3:10 NAS) Thank-you, Jesus. Amen

Words build or tear down. Build your soul on the foundation of His Words and you will have a less troublesome life.

Now take a moment to make a list of His words about you. This is the beginning of building your foundation upon the Rock. Here's a short list to get you going:

> I am His beloved.
> He is my righteousness.
> I am the lost sheep that was found.
> As He is in heaven, so am I in this world.
> Nothing can separate me from the love of God.
> I am fearfully and wonderfully made.

Begin to confess Gods truth over yourself. Like the soul in the story, you will begin to integrate, spirit, soul and body as you begin to believe what He says about you.

(GEN. 49:17; Ps. 140:3; Ps 58::3,4; PROV. 6:2; 18:21; 21:23; Is. 6:5; LUKE 6:4 NKJV; PHIL. 3:10)

The Sixth Wall

Hope Deferred

"Hope deferred makes the heart sick;
Hope fulfilled is a tree of Life."

Prov. 13:12

After abiding for a good long while, we began again, for many walls remained to be overcome. Surprised, I find that not only have we taken a right turn around the mountain, but we are also connected at the hip. Our steps are congruent and I no longer look at the ground for sure-footedness. Each step is his step. Now I can focus on what's ahead. I can also see my beloved's head as he looks on toward our goal.

Amazingly, I can turn in all directions, even while we are walking forward and never lose step with him. It reminds me of Ezekiel's wheel within a wheel. He never loses his focus, and I am never separated from him or out of step.

This trip around the mountain is a smooth dirt road. I have never been here before. Even though I know another wall is coming up, I am not in fear. I am immersed in joy for my heart is full and I now know that whatever dangers and suffering might lie ahead, he is more than able to take care of me.

This desert road has become a time of happy solitude. I am learning the pleasant nature of my own company, coupled with His felt presence. He does not speak, nor do I. However, it is not awkward, as with strangers, for we are not strangers. He is more familiar to me, than I am with myself. I have not, on the other hand, known myself very well. But together we are quite comfortable with that familiarity of peace between us and the history we share. But the road is getting more and more narrow and our right side, the side I am attached to, is exposed to the jagged drop-off. With feet dangling over the edge, I am forced to trust him with my survival. And I dare not look down. Fear has already crept in with imaginations, bringing along bodily feelings of falling. So, I close my eyes and focus inwardly upon him. I settle my soul into the rhythmic movement of his gait, like a baby cradled at the breast, rocking in her mother's arms.

Around the bend, a 20-foot red brick wall appeared. We cannot pass, for it crossed the entire road. Great dread filled me as I considered having to back down the mountain on that skinny dirt road.

Just as this image was being built in my mind, I beheld his maneuvering a turnabout. Mind you, this road is only as wide as he is. First with right front hoof, placed behind right rear hoof, his mid-section folded up like an accordion. With his tail now flat against the mountain wall, he quite easily fashioned our turnabout the rest of the way.

Pressed between the donkey and the mountain, sharp, rocky edges of this circumstance did not cut nor tear me to shreds as one would have thought.

My vision was obscured, I began to think, "What relief it is to know that we will not have to back down the mountainside." Momentary relief turned to disorientation. Bodily, I sensed a shift in direction. We were backing up! To my surprise, a gate was hidden in the wall, painted in the artist's style of trompe loiel. The deception of paint was to discourage Donkeys, Unicorns and others from advancing through the obstacle, but, why backwards? He could have avoided the dangerous turnabout and just walked in. For the first time during our adventure, Unicorn spoke to me in the midst of the Donkey. It was as if he had heard my pondering thoughts. "Darling, this is the sentimentality of fulfilled and beautiful memories and hopes deferred for dreams yet unfulfilled. They must be left behind so that the pain of memory and perceptions of loss be not elevated in the mind." He had read my mind once again! He had heard my questioning thoughts pertaining to his decision to enter backwards. In this I learned to ask him questions, and not to disregard his presence with me, for this is an arrogant lie, a belief that I am alone. But more than this, he knew my heart. I could not have known what would soon transpire within my own depths.

Now that I was positioned against the mountain, I could not turn like a wheel in every direction. My vision was temporarily darkened, due to the precious donkey on the outside. I was thoroughly surrounded by his presence and unable to see that which would have destroyed my ability to finish my journey.

I was kept completely in peace during the transition to the other side. It wasn't until he turned around, once through the gate, that the wheel-like motion was no longer frozen. I wheeled around to see where we had passed through. Though we were in a wide and vast country, I scarcely noticed. For the vision of the back- side of the wall devastated my heart.

It was like tarnished pewter with tormented faces molded into it. I prayed, "Oh my God! No, no! God, no!" Teeth chattering at the horror of it, tears hot with passion, I wailed and wailed that anguished silent scream with no words at all. Intense pain rolled in waves of physical revulsion from the depths of where all things emanate. Sounds, like that of an ocean within a hollow sea conch, echo the empty womb of what could have been. With the panting of a woman in travail, I wondered what would be born. My comprehension was anesthetized. Caught in the timeless travail between heavenly reality and earthly pain, something was being created. Would it be a stillbirth? I knew somehow, it had to do with my lifetime vow to love, honor and cherish, and I was so grieved. So I prayed to God to change his outcome, our outcome.

All this time the donkey waited.

This travail and grief was deep within, as if it had been there for a long time. The donkey was patient, not hurrying me along. Though he is compassionate, he is not comforting me. Perhaps this is a process, which must, of nature, be painful and mixed through time. Some things cannot be rushed. It is reminiscent of the maiden in Song of Solomon whose belly is like a heap of wheat that is full of mixed wine. The wheat being our spiritual offspring, our seeds brought to harvest. And perhaps the mixture in her belly is the mixed blessing of travail, painful, yet fruitful.

Though the time seemed lengthy, the donkey did not sit. He stood, as if over-seeing as a midwife.

Sorrowful, still heavy in my being, I recalled how the Unicorn continued on, even though courage was yet to be manifested in his heart. Desiring to be like that beautiful One at the second wall, I turned from the tarnished pewter wall with head lifted high. Yet the donkey did not move.

Again he spoke to me saying, "This is different, Darling. Don't be like Ephraim, the unwise son, who though the pains of childbirth came upon him, he would not travail to bring forth. It is not the time that he should delay at the opening of the womb. You can change his outcome and yours into this wide and vast land. Change his torment into joy."

So I turned again to the tarnished pewter wall, and looked upon it's pain, which was really his and mine. And again I wept. My spine straightened, and I reached out to touch the tormented faces. In so doing, they slid downward, as if the pewter melted into the ground. As it disappeared, a transparent glass was revealed from beneath the pewter. The gate below could now be plainly seen for what it was, a gate of transparency, humility.

I felt myself lay down inside, as if tired from the travail. I am still greatly aware that I am frail and in need of physical rest. It was then when that docile Donkey cuddled me and just let me cry. His gentle compassion comforted me. I totally let down and melted further into the safety of his nurture.

There is no thought or concern, no excitement or anticipation to explore the new mysterious wide and vast land. In fact, I have scarcely noticed this new land waiting to be pioneered. I am only by the side of the road, as Rachel was after her death, crying for her children, natural and spiritual.

"This travail brought about the demise of sentimentality, which idolizes the past, and torments the present with deferred hope for the future, making the heart sick. The transparency revealed the door of passage to a promised land, which you have yet to comprehend. Many seeds of hope will be planted in this next season."

"Hope," Darling whispered under her breath, "That's something I have not been able to do for some years, now."

Unicorn replied, "Four small letters carry so much weight. H-O-P-E. Without this collection of letters in this sequence, however, mankind would give up and fall asleep forever."

I pondered his words, right there beside the transparent gate. I noticed that looking back through the glass, I can now see without suffering how narrow the path had been. I also recounted the steps and the fear associated with the sharp cliff. I marveled that we had made it to the gate at all. Because of the transparent window, all things became as they truly are. And somehow, there was still safety. I had thought the enemy would destroy what he could see, what was in plain sight. But the opposite was true. What was easily seen was untouchable. It's what we hide from the eyes of the Lover of our soul, and from our self, that gives the enemy legal ground. In hiding, self-protection manifests itself as fear of being found-out, fear of being vulnerable and the pride of unbelief, an evil heart.

Turning within the wheel to face forward again, I beheld a miraculous thing! Right there before my eyes, in this season of vastness, the unicorn sloughed-off his donkey coat, which draped elegantly around his single horn. This was done so that he could be seen for what he was, no disguises. The power of intercession transformed the cloak of the burden-bearer. Instead of leaving it beside the transparent gate, he kept it, as if it were a sentimental token, or so I thought. Perhaps he wanted to remember what it was like to bear so many burdens, or maybe to remind him to slough off burdens before they rob the joy of hope. Whatever the reason, I became confused by the saving of the donkey cloak, since the wall of sentimentality was destroyed. Surely he must have known my confusion, since he seems to read my thoughts. But he did not address me in any fashion. He simply moved forward.

My heart still heavy, I noticed saddlebags upon his back. They were very old and looked like something more appropriate for the donkey to wear instead of the unicorn. They were filled with seed, ancient seed from the Garden of Eden. Each seed seemed to have life and personality, mingled with excitement for their season to arrive. They had been waiting for the appointed time to be cast into the ground, to bear fruit after their own kind. The transparent wall made me think of this vast land like a greenhouse, though it was open everywhere, except at the glass wall. All was dirt, but nice, dark, fertile dirt, plowed from the period of intercession. It was waiting to be planted, impregnated.

I reached into the bag and like a whirlybird, spun around dispersing the seed in circles. He moved slowly at first, since I was still lagging behind in deferred hope, which had been like a pool of quicksand, drinking up my joy. But then as we continued twirling in circles, the heaviness of heart turned into frolicking joy. He began bounding about as I spread the seed. In doing so, his feet kicked up the soft dirt, covering the broadcast seed.

Once again, it was labor without labor. And I noticed that for the first time, this was a work we accomplished together.

Covering the whole territory, which was vast, our bags were now empty. I wondered what the seeds would grow to be, for they were many various kinds. As I pondered this, a soft rain began and we stood in its freshness, eyes closed. Satisfaction entered my heart. Tears began to mingle with raindrops upon my cheeks, for a pang of memory surfaced, overshadowing my joy. I began to reminisce about the hardships of life and the unspeakable suffering that had been my bed. In the heat of it all, I could only lie down and be immersed in life's sufferings. Like satin sheets, never comfortable, either too hot or too cold, conforming to the temperature of the surrounding air, I had resigned myself to accept my circumstances as God's work, but not really. If I had accepted instead of resigned, I would have had the strength of joy to carry on and hope for the future. Resignation only robs one of joy, which is strength.

I thought, "Here I am in a new land and the promise of new life in the seeds, which I myself broadcast into the ground of a hopeful heart. It seems bittersweet, now, and my heart cannot apprehend excitement. Familiar feelings flare and I am tempted to believe that I will always feel this way."

Just then, a certain seed caught my eye. It had missed the covering of fresh dirt and lay exposed to the air, a scenario that would mean shallow roots and a shortened life span. It was larger than all the other seeds and had alternating gray and yellow vertical stripes. Very thin frays of its composition crowned the tip, reminding me of the silk of an ear of corn or a birthday party hat finished off with a delicate plume of festive flare.

Somehow, I felt more love for this seed than all of the others. Perhaps because of its vulnerability, my heart rushed to its rescue. The flow of motherhood touched my emotion. I was moved with concern for its survival, its very life. With a profound knowing, I knew that this particular one was a significant part of my life. Without it, none of the others would flourish.

Looking across the freshly planted expanse, a solitary tree came into view. Quite carefully, I positioned the seed under the farthest extending bough of that trees' canopy, making sure adequate sunlight and protective shade were in equal parts. It was one last seed for future's destiny. Patting the dirt covering, as one pleased with her accomplishment, I realized the heaviness had disappeared. Still, I wondered what that seed would be.

With satisfaction in my heart, I was ready to move on to the next place. But the Unicorn just lingered. Something else significant was here, but I couldn't ascertain it and I was growing agitated with impatience. Instead of sensing a forth-coming event, which would have filled me with the fear of holiness, I wanted to move on and get through the next walls. This attitude revealed a certain amount of humility still needing to be developed within my character; a willingness to wait for Unicorns' leading.

It was then that I paid attention to the directives of my senses. For feelings always point us to face the truth, if we will only stop to notice and question. Not that feelings are always right, but they are always truthful, betraying the seat or bottom of what we really believe; the deep beliefs, faults and truths that lurk beneath the surface of our consciousness.

A certain sadness emanated from the Unicorn. But before I could fully settle into this acknowledgment, he abruptly turned, running headlong into the glass wall. It all shattered into shards, falling into one big heap at the side of the road. It was to be a reminder that sentimentality can be a torment in the memory of looking back through the past; that even the good character of transparency can be a wall of glass between people when used without wisdom; and worse yet, is the effect of lost communion with the Lover of our Soul. No barrier, not even transparent glass can stand between, or else we are doomed to remain two, never to merge as One, together.

At this understanding, I was quieted inside. And the Unicorn was released to move forward for the next part of our journey.

(Prov. 13:12; Ez. 1:6; Hosea 13:13)

Between the Walls

He Is Our Hope

Sentimentality is governed by feelings. It keeps one stuck in the past. Sentimentality idolizes the past and its fulfilled dreams and happy times. It torments the present with depression, sadness, pain of the mind, and builds evil expectation, which produces more hope deferred for a future of unfulfilled desire and dreams. Sentimentality postpones the fruit of perseverance.

Sentimentality can be a form of dissociation. It is a refuge for one to avoid the current circumstances of life. If left in this state, you lose your whole life's potential.

Sometimes the Author and Finisher of our lives causes the path you are on to narrow in order to cause you to run out of escape options from something He wants you to look at. So, circumstances may become harder, no grace may be found in a relationship or work situation, finances, health, stress all around. As your outward options are totally removed, you may find yourself stuck. But inwardly you still have a choice: to choose *dissociation*, a form of escape isolated from the Lord, or to choose *association*, with the Lord, making Him your strong tower of protection. This second choice is the direction the Lord wants you to take.

Dissociation can be clearly seen as the Donkey stands while the soul turned a different direction. At first, the soul was acting separately from its' body. The Donkey was moved to intercession, but the soul rationalized a different solution to the crisis. Soul remembered a time when the Holy Spirit sacrificed His own desire for the good of others. The soul saw it as emotionally courageous. Desiring to be like Him, Darling began to walk away from the circumstance. But Donkey felt intercession rising bodily.

The Darling soul chose association by looking at the painful memories, which tormented her. The happy ones were the worst because the days of that happiness were gone. Nothing but hard times and frustration were her present life. Hope for anything good had evaded her and she was left with hope deferred until another season of life.

But once again, she chose association with the Lover of her soul by allowing the memories and their emotion to surface. Instead of repressing them, she listened to the wisdom in her body and its' inclination. She interceded, prayed in the spirit with the deepest part of her being. She could have dissociated and pushed down the emotions like Ephraim in Hosea 13. Instead she listened to the Unicorn's leading, which was to allow the fullness of her pain, sorrow and grief to surface. This act acknowledges the pieces of your soul and the work they have carried out for you by storing, perhaps forgotten memories, which carried the trauma. At this narrow road, it is time to face, release and redeem your past. If you continue to repress your pain, it will come out at inappropriate times and sometimes in unlovely ways. Be good to yourself and take the time to cry out those gut-wrenching and silent cries, like a woman in travail, giving birth, because you are giving birth to parts of yourself that need to be relieved from their burdens.

To continue holding on to such pain will cause hope to die and the death of many un-birthed, unborn dreams and desires. All of this amounts to your destiny!

(Prov. 13:12; Ps. 42:5; 42:11;; 1John 3:3)

100 Fold: The Deeper Story

Hope deferred makes the heart sick (worn, weak, afflicted, pain, infirmity), which drives the soul into intercession. Intercession releases sickness of heart and sows seed for future harvests. It is one method of integrating and produces hope fulfilled, which is a Tree of Life (prosperity in your soul, health for your body and produces the fruit of perseverance. Prov. 13:12).

During intercession, we enter into the Holy of Holies within the temple of our body. We take hold of the horns of the altar, lying upon the Mercy Seat and depositing our deepest pain, fears and disappointments from hope deferred. Upon completion of our souls' release, we are transformed from the burden-bearer to the covering cherub who guards the entrance to the Garden of Eden, God's Throne within you. It is a threshold moving from the Holy Place (of the 60 Fold), into the Holy of Holies (the 100 Fold) All such activity is holy to the Lord, because of the sacrifice of one's will to the obedience of Christ. It is the sacrifice of your dissociating ways. Spirit, soul and body working together in intercession crucifies the dissociative habit, thus healing the fragmented pieces of the soul pertaining to the circumstances that brought on the intercession. All that were isolated in the memories of the tormented faces and sentimentality were released of their burdens. As the darling soul rested, cuddled within the Donkey, a metaphor for the body, an integration with her own body was facilitated. With some souls who have endured much trauma, many integrations are required.

Intercession in the deep groanings of the Spirit facilitates integration. This is a profound working of the Spirit within a lover of God and is one tool He uses to heal us. The many seeds sown in intercession will grow into a full harvest of God's promises to you. In that day, you will rejoice in the Tree of Life, Himself, who is Christ in you, the hope of Glory! (Col. 1:27)

The knowledge soon comes to the soul, that He is our hope. We have been desiring vain (empty) things. If we focus on Him and run "into" Him instead of self-protection in a dissociated piece of our soul, we will find everything we need: peace, protection; safety, security, abundance, prosperity, love and all of the fruit of the Spirit.

It's important to know that the soul tries to organize the Spirit; to make methods and patterns to follow in every circumstance. But each circumstance is unique and the Spirit knows all things. When soul is submitted to Holy Spirit, the soul is a masterful tool. If the Spirit is an artist, with a vision and plan, then the soul is the brush in the artists' hand. And the body is the painting, a manifestation of the soul and Spirit, doing only those things that it sees the Heavenly Father doing.

(PROV. 13:12; COL. 1:27; JOHN 5:19)

The Seventh Wall

Intimidation

INSIDE MYSELF, I WAS SINGING A NEW SONG I HAD never heard before, "The time is now! All things are possible, now! Don't wait. This is the time." As I sang and twirled about in the wheel within the wheel, I noticed that the unicorn had taken on servant hood, again. The Donkey re-emerged and he was somber. I felt a knot form in his stomach, like the pit of a peach.

Excitement settled into apprehension. And I was internally reminded of the job at hand…to tear down walls.

The wide, vast land narrowed to a dirt road with a bend up ahead. The closer we came to that bend, the more apprehension filled my mind. Not knowing the future can lend itself to many a great fantasy of the mind, not necessarily happy ones.

Worry and fear are the bridges to painful expectations. But the child thereof is what was expected.

Rounding the bend, there stood in animated, human form, another wall, which tried to intimidate us. The donkey never engaged its eyes, but in a meek manner, sidestepped its advances. Strange enough, this wall moved and seemed to have life and thought, but its foundation was grounded in sand, making it lame to walk. It was like a child's inflatable Bobo doll, containing a sand-filled bottom.

Still a brick and mortar wall, each brick took the appearance of liquid metal. Each time the form leaned out toward us, another feature would be revealed. It became obvious that the form's hands could not separate from nor act independently from the rest of the wall. Therefore, its hands could not capture us. And, even though the expression of the liquid metal face was angry and aggressive, it had no teeth!

Having no feet, no hands and no teeth, I wondered why we acted so cowardly by not looking it square in the eyes and tearing it down. Once having that thought, I realized that its power was released by the intimidation of its eyes. To let it look into the eyes, the window of the soul, intimidation's power could easily overthrow the strongest of hearts. Overcoming this beast requires one to not only appear meek and non-threatening, but to remain in the knowledge that pride will bring even the greatest to ruin. Humility is the answer again.

To this point, it is significant to note that the donkey's heart was still brave and strong, though he respected the powerful possibilities of his enemy, intimidation. He did not falter in the heart. He knew intimidation had no teeth. And it was expedient to dress in ordinary fashion, thus reserving Unicorn's radiant beauty for those who would not be incited by his purity. For no one in the flesh is impressed with a donkey, that humble beast of burden. And no one desires his ordinary appearance that of a servant, except those wise in heart. Vanity is truly empty and only temporarily satisfying. To desire outward beauty is human. But to *be* beauty is to have obtained humility. It is irresistible to those who are of noble heart. Many who lust after beauty desire to rise above others in a competitive spirit. Some seek it at great cost and exchange the priceless and eternal gold of humility for the grand prize of pride, frolicking for the lust of men. The greatest cost, of course, is the forfeiture of Oneness with the

Lover of your soul. For many of His finest souls are cloaked in humble exteriors. This is a protection from elevating oneself above one's fellows. Those souls who are born with a natural beauty also have many obstacles to overcome. Some obstacles are the obvious temptation to seduce and manipulate others for personal gratification. Another is the danger of outside predators inhabiting the bodies of men pursuing their own lustful gratification. The latter is a leading cause of the splitting and shattering of precious young souls in the first place.

In case you are wondering, as did I, this reappearance of the donkey's coat was no betrayal of truth. For the donkey's coat was still attached at the horn, and his heart was truly humble.

As the donkey's demeanor continued along these lines, the wall began to shrink. It lost its power the more the donkey persisted.

Finally, the wall was overcome and shrank to no more than an inch or two high. That's when, with one sure-footed hoof, the donkey simply stepped on the shrunken wall. And as quick as that, the wall was gone. Not even rubble remained. "Sometimes the way up is down."

(1 Pet. 5:8; Jer. 16:19; Is 57:13; Eccl. 1:2)

Between the Walls

Sometimes the way up is down

A BOBO DOLL IS AN INFLATABLE PUNCHING BAG, which sits on the ground and has a sand-filled base. Each time it is hit it bounces back to an upright position. You could say that it's relentless but predictable. Intimidation, which can arise out of pride or fear, is much the same way. Whether you intimidate others or you are easily intimidated, this wall needs to come down.

This wall is so deceptive in that it is built upon pride, which is based upon self-righteousness. Like the liquid metal wall, pride takes many forms. In our story, the Bobo doll was grounded in sand. According to Luke 7:24-27, we can either build our soul on the rock of Christ, believing what He says and doing what He tells us to do; or we can build it on the foundation of sand by not acknowledging

Him, which brings deep insecurity for our soul. Take a moment and read Luke 7:24-27.

A sandy foundation quickly washes out when the storms of life occur. So, as you are integrating your soul, you may find areas of belief that are untrue, that have created a faulty foundation. These must be torn down and rebuilt upon the Rock of Truth, who is Christ Jesus.

Ask Holy Spirit to show you areas of a faulty foundation, where you've built your beliefs upon something other than the Truth about yourself or God or others, not your "truth" or any other "truth." Truth, Himself, is the only unchangeable, absolute. His Truth is the foundation built upon the Rock. When troubles arise in your life, the Rock of His word will keep you from falling.

All souls are burdened with some sort of insecurities. Most separations from God, otherwise known as sin, are caused by one of two things: Pride or Fear. Both create insecurities within the soul. Pride usually rises up from this sandy foundation and forms a technique of protection from a perceived danger or threat to the souls belief of who it is. Pride is a method of protection for the false identity, that which the soul wrongly believes about itself. It sidesteps the protection of the Lord. We are told to run into His Spirit when we are threatened, but our pattern of self-defense is usually by way of fight, flight or freeze. This is the triggered response of the lowest part of the brain, the brain stem or amygdala. Some call it the lizard brain. These methods are great when our physical life is threatened. But the Spirit of God calls us to come up to a higher perspective with Him. Until the soul decides to let go of its habit of finding protection in the lower part of the soul, and trust Him instead, it remains immature and distanced from the Lover of the soul. Left undisciplined it will overtake the entire soul, growing from a small lizard into a giant dragon, the beast of Revelation. Humility is the answer to overcoming the pride of running to other methods of protection. "If my people which are called by my name, shall humble themselves and pray and seek my face, and turn from their wicked ways; then will I hear from heaven, and will forgive their sin, and heal their land." 2 Chronicles 7:14. By definition, humility is the absence of pride.

TAKE ACTION

It is helpful to know the personal method you use to protect yourself when you feel threatened. Begin to notice your emotions and reactions inside yourself. Once you make this a habit of discovery, your progress will come more quickly. For example, when you feel put-down or disrespected, if you clam-up and can't think of a thing to say, you may be using the freeze (also called feigning death) response. If under the same scenario your anger rises and lashes out, this may be the fight response. Or if you have a strong drive to just leave the conversation, hang-up the phone or run away, it could be the flight response.

It is a wise soul that asks Holy Spirit to give a check in the spirit when prideful thoughts or behaviors are present. Also, "Casting down imaginations, and every high thing that exalts itself against the knowledge of God, and bringing into captivity every thought to the obedience of Christ." (2 Cor. 10:5), Quickly and immediately replace it with humility, knowing that "…God resists the proud, but gives grace to the humble." (James 4:6). This results in a freedom from the old ways and is the work of the 60-fold company of Christ.

Pride wishes to intimidate you and we are all prone to its effects. If a souls identity is built on a flimsy foundation of sand it will never be an overcomer. In other words, it will never grow into the 100-fold company of Christ. This is called "walking out your salvation with fear and trembling." (see Phil. 2:12)

The word "face" in the Bible is symbolic of presence; the presence of a person or spirit. To look upon the face, then, is to engage in the presence of a person or spirit. This is why Donkey meekly avoided looking directly into the eyes of intimidation. He did not want to engage with that spirit and risk confrontation in an unholy manner. Never argue with pride. Rather, replace the prideful, intimidating thoughts or words with Gods' Word. This act of humility prohibits the liquid metal wall from having any teeth. Speaking metaphorically, it cannot devour you. Pride is disabled.

However, to look it squarely in the face and fight with it will bring a soul down in defeat, even though the soul may believe it won the battle. This is because the real battle is not to win the argument, but to rise above the need to "win" or to be "right," since this is motivated by pride. "Rule thou in the midst of thine enemies." (Ps. 110:2)

Everything is built by our beliefs. Build your foundation upon the Rock of what He says about you. Who does He say that you are?

(Luke 7:24-27; Rev. 4:1; 2 Chron. 7:4; 2Cor. 10:5; James 4:6; Phil.2:12; Ps. 110:2)

100 Fold: The Deeper Story

IN MATTHEW 13, VERSES 18-23, WE FIND THE parable of the sower. Please read then continue in this study.

In verse 23 we find the soul that is "the good ground" and received the word of God and understood. As we first hear, then do the teachings of the Lord, our soul produces fruit. Some people apply the learning and multiply their soul by 30 fold. Others continue and begin to crucify their pride and their soul increases by 60 fold and this is a dramatic leap forward for the soul! Still others dig their well deeper by learning to abide in the Spirit and produce 100 fold. The question is, how deep do you want to be? God will take you as far as you want to go.

As noted above, "face" in the Bible refers to the presence of a person or spirit, whether holy or unholy. After bearing the 60-fold fruit of crucifying the dissociation into the lizard brain, we come to the 100-fold abiding in the presence of Him whom our soul loves because "He who is forgiven much loves much." The soul is beginning to really grasp a deeper understanding of its' depravity and the greatness of His gift to us on the cross. The great losses of false identities worked through Grace produce humility in the soul. Thus causing the soul to fall more deeply in love with its' Savior.

This helps to produce the beauty of holiness, which is purity in the soul as opposed to vanity, which is emptiness in the soul. Emptiness begs to be filled and draws all sorts of bedfellows unto its' self. Upon the repentance and expulsion of vanity, the infilling of the beautiful fruit of holiness abides in the soul. In other words, vanity produces no good fruit in the soul and is a product of pride. It is a competitive spirit that wishes to elevate a soul above other souls, which is an ungodly motive of the heart. Having crucified this ungodly spirit, the beautiful fruit of holiness takes its' place and fills the void of vanity.

This beauty is not natural beauty of the physical appearance. Rather, it is an everlasting beauty of holiness. Purity is another word for holiness. Those souls destined for the 100-fold abiding in

Christ are not necessarily seeking a physical beauty. However the outward showing of the inward fruit of holy purity is clearly seen through the face and discerned by observers.

This beauty causes jealousy in the hearts of unrefined souls and their desire is two-fold: to destroy the holy purity and/or acquire it for themselves sometimes in a physical means by way of unholy sexual behavior, i.e., molestation and rape, fornication and all unsanctified sexual behavior. These unholy actions, of course, can never produce the beauty these predators desire to contain within themselves. For these lusts, stemming from pride must all be crucified in the soul before it can produce the holy purity it seeks to devour in others. God is no respecter of persons. What He has done in one soul He can and will produce in another soul, if the soul so desires. They need only ask. "… you have not because you ask not."

Nonetheless, the physical assaults upon a person can create fractures in the soul. The Lover of the soul has provided a way of complete healing from such fractures.

It is in learning to abide in the Spirit of Him who made us, which sets us free much more quickly.

Whether or not a soul has endured sexual fracturing, the nature of entering into the 100-fold creates a movement that fluctuates between 60-fold and 100-fold. Our process is going in and going out, just like the priests of the tabernacle of Moses. Jesus exhibited this on the Mount of Olives, known as the Mount of Transfiguration under the New Covenant. It is a transfiguration that occurs within the soul, each time it enters the 100 Fold condition, until the fullness of our crucifixion process is complete. Once completed, a soul can abide in the acknowledged presence of God 100% of their remaining days. Of course, backsliding is always a possibility until the soul becomes accustomed to staying in the fortress of the Lord's presence, forfeiting always its' choice to dissociate. The ability to dissociate is always available to the soul if it so desires.

Only the Lord sees this interior progression of the soul and so in the story it is shown as the Donkeys' coat still connected at the horn. This indicates another successful integration of the soul with Spirit and body and an increase in anointing, power and authority.

The horn of the Unicorn is a symbol of power and authority (See Deut. 33:13-17) and the

Donkeys' coat is symbolic of an anointing or call upon a persons' life. As one integrates, anointing and power are increased. It is important to recognize that humility is vital to the growth of good character, anointing, authority and power, for without it the soul would become an undisciplined tyrant to itself and others.

Now close your eyes. Ask for the Lover of your soul to draw you, to deepen you. Ask Him to develop 100-fold fruit in your soul, for His good pleasure. Now, abide for as long as you can.

(Mat. 13:18-23; James 4:2; Deut. 33:13-17)

The Eighth Wall

A Very Small Box

CONTINUING ON, THE INCLINE STEADILY increased as the road bulged out forming a nice wide path, still dirt, still smooth. I could see the unicorn's white fur, mingling in with the donkey's gray. With each conquering step, more of the unicorn's white hair emerged, forming a salt and pepper mixture, as might be compared to a maturing humans hair.

Except for the beginning of the adventure, I have been like a wheel inside of a wheel attached to the Donkey's hip. Now, somehow, I can't see myself anymore. And I am very happy about that! For self-centeredness is a curse. I don't know where I went, but it seems deeper than before. It is at this same moment I realize that he will do as I ask, for he is my servant. This frightening thought was accompanied with a steady stream of physical sensations. First, an unusual shrinking inside, with a visual image of raised eyebrows, as if to say, "What audacity!" followed by a deeper love, as I understood how much more he loves and trusts me, than I love and trust myself. My insides are shaken with self-doubt, as I remember the many mistakes and poor decisions I have made, and I collapse in a deliverance from an unseen wall. Outside eyes were unable to see it, though I knew it was there. It was a fear of reigning and ruling, having dominion over my own life, of taking charge and making decisions for myself. With each thought of commanding the donkey, more internal folding resulted. Like a paper origami box, that wall folded down to a pint size, encapsulated by an aura of fear. It was a square box, within the enlarged road. I couldn't tell exactly where I was within the Donkey. It was a place I'd never been before.

Knowledge without learning spontaneously answered the question I was yearning to ask. What was in the box that needed such a fortress of fear to contain it and keep it from emerging? It was me! My true, self had been abandoned in a box, trusting others to know better than I, what was best for me.

With this revelation came a burst of fire,

filling the box and consuming it. It's flames ignited instantly without a match. The box, which had formed a wall called fear, lost its power, and the origami house was filled with smoke. As a burnt offering goes up in smoke, it is a holocaust of false beliefs and fears of trusting that the Unicorn would lead me in every decision. I was no longer alone in my decision-making. All I had to do was ask.

I rested inside. Plump water droplets containing heavenly words began to water my newly awakened spirit.

Confining boundaries removed, no longer despised and put to sleep, the real me expands with the width of my path; for it's a path requiring the full fire of God's freedom. Never Mind Trail.

(Is. 6:4)

Between the Walls

Passive Fear

PASSIVITY ALLOWS ANYONE AND ANYTHING through the boundary of skin into the holy land of your being. We have been given voice to condemn every tongue that rises against us in judgment, whether through the spirit of a person or through whisperings of a spirit of the air. We are the righteousness of Christ, not our own self-righteousness, which is pride. (See Isaiah 54:17)

Some have given up their own voice, their own choices to another. Some have had their voice taken from them through intimidation or trauma. Whatever the case, you can take your own voice back and to be sure, God wants you take your voice back and use it!

"You have not because you ask not." (James 4:2 NKJV). In this context, asking is not for natural things, finances and health, for example, but for spiritual help, knowledge and wisdom. As part of the same problem of taking dominion over your own "land," take a moment and ask the Lord to help you take your voice back. Ask Him if there is anything you should be asking for in the way of integrating. Then listen. Write down all that comes to you and date it. Then write your progress as it comes and see the answers God gives you. It will encourage you!

(Is. 54:17; James 4:2 NKJV)

100 Fold: The Deeper Story

THE TEMPLE OF GOD, WHOM YOU ARE, HAS three compartments: the outer court, your body; the holy place, your soul (mind, will, emotions, your personality); and the holy of holies, your spirit. For deeper understanding, read about Moses' tabernacle in Exodus 35-38. This gives a picture of your inward temple, a temple made without hands. The Holy of Holies was a 10 x 10 square room (which equals 100 fold). This represents the deepest part of being, your spirit, where the spirit of God dwells within you, if you have asked Him to be your Lord and Savior. It is the smallest room in your being, the temple of God.

In the story, the spirit of the person had been relegated to a very small role, essentially put to sleep. This allowed the soul to rule and reign, being in charge of the entire being, spirit, soul and body. Unfortunately, this is the way most people live their entire lives! But Gods' word says, "For as many as are led by the Spirit of God, they are the sons of God (Romans 8:14). We are to be led by His Spirit, not by our soul, since the latter would lead us back into slavery, which brings fear. A soul in control puts the spirit in bondage.

So, fear is the guardian of the sleeping spirit. And until the person decides to allow the Father to wake it up, it remains shrouded in fear. As soon as the person decides, he or she can be delivered from sleep, thus setting a fire as an holy holocaust.

(Ex. 35-38; Rom. 8:14)

The Ninth & Tenth Walls

Others and an Ancient Key

WE LEFT THE WALL THAT HAD BECOME AN altar of incense. Feeling rather floaty and free, we traveled up the road. Though I wasn't aware of the path or surroundings, I began to feel troubled inside. The Donkey's hair stood on end and his shoulders tensed. I seemed to have lost the Unicorn. This distressed me no end! For I felt emptiness left by His seeming departure as we approached enemy territory. Every part of me wanted His embrace back, but it wasn't to be, for I looked to my right and there He was. Gracefully but with some urgency, Unicorn turned to us handing me an ancient, carved key, saying, "This key will open hearts." All seemed to be focused upon one upcoming event, a confrontation with one of a different gender. In this relationship I, Darling, knew myself as "not loved," although that belief had been with me from my mother's womb.

Along the path, a friendly bird came to feed me with encouragement. I was strengthened with the words, "The Lord intends to do you good. You are not going before *them*; they are coming before *you*!" I then knew there was a hidden agenda plotted against me, as was once against Queen Esther. Nonetheless, my path required overcoming these two obstacles to my destiny.

We came to twin walls that looked like a table; one lay horizontally upon the other vertical and they sat on the edge of a cliff. One relied upon the other for stability and they grew in strength with their verbal banter. Together they formed an unfriendly table, each with a face and a very large mouth. With each sentence they spoke a plate of food appeared, familiar food I had eaten many times before. It was, as it were, a table of communion, an unholy alliance, witnessed by two.

In unison, the Donkey and I moved to sit at the table, for we are now in one accord, one unit bodily, a witness of two. "A thousand shall fall at your side and ten-thousand at your right hand, but it shall not come near you." Without thought, reason or hesitation, we just moved, as if caught by a current of water. This was unusual, for just a wall before I would not have acquiesced.

The tables' banter filled the air and I felt as if I was the meal to be consumed. Looking around, I sought to see what the Unicorn was doing. Without seeing a vision or dreaming a dream of Him, I didn't know what to do. I had become accustomed to seeing and following His lead as I could always mimic His behavior. But I couldn't find Him as in the past. I felt alone in the company of these two. Had Unicorn abandoned me? Prior to the last healing, I would have panicked, trying to work it out logically. But no such fear this time. I found that although I felt alone I also felt a curious courage, for a mysterious internal embrace accompanied me within my heart.

In the midst of this pondering, I again realized the current situation. It began to reveal the essence of loss pertaining to a human relationship. I did not cower in fear, but used the humility I learned at the seventh wall. Without thinking, I opened my heart to the Other. When I did, that mysterious internal embrace flowed out. I was overcome with a warm, peaceful power, filling me from the top of my head, flowing throughout my being. I received it first for myself, then directed it to the Other, whom I had once seen as an enemy. Since the internal box was no longer there shielding me from receiving love, I exercised my inexperienced and youthful freedom by letting the warmth flow through me like a river. As I was vulnerable I became strong with boundaries. It was then that a miraculous thing happened! *The Other's* wall of ice melted straight away. Tenderness filled his eyes and voice. As the Other's heart flowed toward me the internal vertical wall that formed the base of the table uprooted it's rebar from within the mortar of my belly, delivering me from the toxic food of "not loved." Mystery solved! This flowing warmth filled not only me, but the Other, as well. Humility opened the door for Love to displace "not loved."

Without a leg to stand on, its twin wall, "insignificant," began to crumble. As it cried out its' pain, the Unicorn reappeared. His compassionate countenance lifted up to the heavenly realm. His intercession looked like my grief poured out into the heavenly realm. Quickly after that, I felt lighter than ever before. No longer would I eat the bread of "insignificant" and "not loved." For they had been transformed into "significant" and "loved." The table within remained in my belly and became a servant delivering the Bread of Heavenly Love and Significance to fellow travelers of all nations. The Other and I cried for the beauty of love's effect. I knew, then, that The Beloved loves me as much as all Others.

Once I stopped eating the bread of "insignificant" and "not loved" I noticed that Donkey's belly was greatly reduced in size. The Unicorn offered an answer to my unspoken observation: "The Heavenly Bread of Love nourishes the soul so the body needn't be expanded with the lying food of 'insignificant'."

This was the ancient key given to me by the Unicorn.

(Ps. 91:7)

Between the Walls

"Love covereth all sins" Prov. 10:12

"Insignificant" and "not loved" are relieved of their duties, which included taking the brunt of all words and signals conveying those messages to the fragmented soul. Darling's "truth" had been that she was insignificant and not loved. This belief had really been with her from the womb. The thoughts and emotions of the mother are imposed upon the child and are passed on through the generations. As Darling's pieces are relieved of the lies she believed, they are renewed and established again into their true identity. Integration is so easy as they automatically are received back into the fold, re-connecting the whole soul, piece by piece. "And ye shall know the truth and the truth shall make you free," (John 8:32).

Imagine the Creator of your soul piecing together a puzzle, which is your soul; mind, will and emotions, which together make a total of your personality. Imagine a puzzle that is partially pieced together, with a few pieces singularly placed around the outside of the otherwise connected puzzle. The puzzle is a picture with a story to tell, but there are blank spots (of memory) where the necessary piece is unconnected, isolated and on the outside. The picture wants to be whole, connected. And the separated pieces want to fit in, no longer alone and lonely. They are waiting for the Master to pick them up, piece by piece. His loving gaze evaluates each one. With purpose, He turns and massages each piece to cause it to wake-up, to find its' purpose, its' place in the whole puzzle so the picture becomes more clear and able to tell the story it was intended to tell. This is the greatness of His gentle love for your soul. Take a moment and return His gaze by acknowledging Him with love from your own heart to His.

> *Father, as you gently and lovingly wake-up the longing pieces of my soul, I rest assured that you love me and desire me to be whole. Though I don't feel Your presence, by faith I know You are here with me and are embracing me with your Spirit hug. I choose to associate with You,*

again. May I always choose You over dissociation! Oh, Lover of my soul. Teach me to be one with you as in John 17.

I give my imagination over to You to use in this life. Purify it and use it for your purposes. I thank-you, Father, that I am covered in the blood of Jesus and your constant gaze is upon me, for I am the apple of your eye and you hide me under the shadow of Thy wings. (paraphrased Ps. 17:8)

Having prayed this prayer, it is a good time to allow the Holy Spirit to minister to you from Psalm 139:15-18:

> *15 "My substance was not hid from thee, when I was made in secret, and curiously wrought in the lowest parts of the earth.*
>
> *16 Thine eyes did see my substance, yet being unperfect; and in thy book all my members were written, which in continuance were fashioned, when as yet there was none of them.*
>
> *17 How precious also are thy thoughts unto me, O God! How great is the sum of them!*

18 If I should count them, they are more in number than the sand: when I awake, I am still with thee."

Imagine yourself as an infant within your mother's womb. Can you imagine God's hands forming you, weaving you together and nurturing you as you are cushioned inside the depths of the "earth" of your mother? Where no human eyes can see, He can see. Darkness is not dark to Him. He has authored your life and written every day in a book all about you! Let yourself experience this profound intimacy He has with you. He knows everything. Nothing is hidden from Him, who loves you inside and out. Bask in His love, in His favor. You are "fearfully and wonderfully made." As you allow Holy Spirit to minister to you, ask Him to remove the deep wound of "insignificance" and "not loved," if they are part of your prenatal package of untruths. Any other untruths' that surface while in this exercise, ask for their removal.

(1Pet. 4:8 NAS; John 8:32; John 17; Ps. 17:8; Ps. 139:15-18)

100 Fold: The Deeper Story

As a soul draws nearer to the Lover by overcoming walls of dissociation, the river of Life flows through it more and more freely, touching others with just their presence in a room. Love has a way of doing that! It disarms the angry man; disrupts hateful thoughts; soothes rejected souls; delights the bearer of good news.

This is the table of communion called the Bread of Heavenly Love and Significance. We are to be "bread to the nations" and although this is a global call, it is also a personal call to heal the imagi*nations*. The beautiful side effect is that many times, the souls' void of love, once filled, can stop being filled with unnecessary food to the belly; For the food of insignificance and not loved holds spiritually empty calories, making one fat, but not with the Spirit.

It is important to know that the carrier of this table must first receive the service of Heavenly Love and Significance before it can be dispersed to others. So, please, re-member your pieces by facing the pain, releasing it and receiving the love of God. Now, rest in His presence and let His love restore your soul.

Integration occurs much more quickly when you spend your time resting in His presence.

(Ps. 23)

The Eleventh Wall

A Crowd on a Foggy Day

Now the Unicorn is on a plateau on the side of the mountain where the Table of Unholy Alliances had been. Twin waterfalls flow perpetually from the cliff's edge reminding us to flow like the Rivers of Living Water. Sparkling and clear, this water refreshes the mountain trees and the sons of God who visit there. The Unicorn is whiter than anything I have ever seen. And he's very happy. It's as if He has a secret, knowing something we don't yet know, and He is not telling.

Through a cloudy, thin fog, I see a banqueting table is set before Him, filled with food to share. A meal is set before him. Crystal goblets rimmed in gold, bone china and silver grace the table. Many more places are set, 20 perhaps. He holds up a teacup and motions toward me. The cup is almost paper thin and opaque as it is held up to the light.

I could see the vulnerability of it as it was cupped within his palms. So fragile is its make-up. I sense there is deeper meaning to this, but I cannot grasp its relevance. He invites us in, but we cannot come in, due to the surrounding fog, a wall I had not recognized as such before. So, He sits alone.

I inquired as to why this solitary meal. What is this foggy wall? It's because his friends are hindered by the cares of the world. It's a wall of hindrance from communing. It keeps us busy, separated and alone. Though he's happy for the great freedom from the previous walls' demise, he will remain alone if we don't take action soon.

Moved with grief, I wailed and interceded for him. I couldn't bear the thought of him being alone and lonely. All I wanted to do was rush to his side and hug Him, eat with Him and just bask in His presence. But no communion was possible as long as those nagging enemies surrounded me. I was fraught with worry. "What can I do?"

Pacing side to side, a sharp thought entered my mind bringing clarity. I could confront the Crowd of Cares one by one, and put them in their place. As soon as I had the thought, the Donkey began to move toward the Crowd. More and more I discovered his keen ability to respond to my thoughts as soon as I have them. It's as if he reads my mind, too. His shoulders were tense and he walked with a tight gait. I can feel his aches and pains and paying close attention, I can sort of "hear" what he is saying. By this I mean to say that he, that beast of burden, seems to have more intelligence than I gave him credit for. Hmm.

The first in the Crowd of Cares was a worry about time and how long it was taking me to overcome these walls. As I looked this Care straight in the eyes, I thought, "My times are in Your hands, oh Lord." Immediately, that foggy Care rolled away. Our shoulders relaxed.

Quickly the Cares came to mind one by one. And one by one they were each addressed in like manner. I could feel the lightness from within the Donkey. Rolling the Crowd of Cares onto Him was much lighter than carrying them. An added effect was that Donkey's aches and pains diminished with each Care we rolled off. Finally, all the fog had cleared and we had no Crowd to separate us from communing with that Beautiful One. This was Unicorn's secret…to roll my cares upon Him, because He cares for me.

I saw Unicorn lift his eyes to the hills, from where our help comes. Then he spoke regarding the teacup made of bone china. He said that it represents me, the darling soul of our being. Just then our Maker broke into the conversation and said, "I made you fragile for Me. For Myself I made you fragile as this bone china teacup. You must rely on Me for strength, for love, for purpose, for direction, for needs, for all things. For the soul of mankind is fragile. My Spirit leads you into all truth. When the soul is burdened by the cares of this world, it lifts out of my hands to do it's own will and work. These burdens are too heavy for a fragile teacup. Soon it cracks and cannot hear My voice. Simply come to Me as you saw the Unicorn doing. He is My spirit within you. Follow Me and I will lead you into all truth."

We lifted our goblets and drank in remembrance of Him and all that He has taught us. Communion was never sweeter.

Between the Walls

Fretting Leprosy

D ONKEY, THE BODY, IS BURDENED DOWN WITH many things, because Darling, the soul, is worried about many things. It is "the sin of worry; anxiety; carefulness; bitterness" (Leviticus 13:51-52; 14:34-45). Kelly Varner in his book Understanding Types, Shadows, and Names explains:

"A leper was a person who suffered from a slowly progressing and incurable skin disease. "Fretting" is from the Hebrew *ma'ar* (Strong's #3992) meaning "to be bitter, or (causitively) to embitter, be painful." It is also rendered in the King James Version as "picking." The Greek word for "bitterness" is *pikria* (Strong's #4088), which means "acridity (especially poison)." Compare *pikros* (Strong's #4089), which means "(through the idea of piercing) sharp (pungent), acrid."

"Careful" is from the Hebrew *charad* (Strong's

2729), which means "to shudder with terror; hence, to fear; also to hasten (with anxiety)." Compare *da'ag* (Strong's #1672), which means "anxious." The Greek word is *phrontizo* (Strong's #5431), meaning "to exercise thought, be anxious." Taken from *phren* ("mind"), it also means "to think, consider, be thoughtful." Compare *merimnao* (Strong's #3309), which means "to be anxious about." Rendered as "take thought" in the King James Version, the latter is taken from *merimna* (Strong's #3308), which means "(through the idea of distraction); solicitude."

Luke 10:38-42 is an account of the sisters, Mary and Martha:

> *38 "Now it came to pass as they went, that he entered into a certain village: and a certain woman named Martha received him into her house.*
>
> *39 And she had a sister called Mary, which also sat at Jesus' feet, and heard his word.*
>
> *40 But Martha was **cumbered** about much serving, and came to him, and said, Lord, dost*

thou not care that my sister hath left me to serve alone? Bid her therefore that she help me.

*41 And Jesus answered and said unto her, Martha, Martha, thou art **careful** and **troubled** about many things:*

42 But one thing is needful: and Mary hath chosen that good part, which shall not be taken away from her."

We, like Martha, can become bitter due to life responsibilities, cares of this world, people we see as burdens, or false responsibilities we take upon ourselves. It is a slow "death," just like leprosy, and causes us much mental pain, reaching the extreme level of anxiety attacks, which demonstrate as a heart attack. In the spiritual sense, it is an attack upon the heart! Who do you choose to honor in each moment? Will you sit at the feet of Jesus or remain in the distractive state of dissociated, anxious, terrorizing fears from your thoughts? The only way through anxiety, bitterness, worry and terror is to repent of these sins, break the generational curses, forgive all people you are angry with, break all inner vows, cry out all bitter roots, cast off and away the spirit of fear, terror and trauma.

Take some time now to do this important enlargement of your soul. This may take some time to complete, but it's vital to your growth and happiness. Give God the space you are making for Him. He will bless you for your every effort to acknowledge Him.

(LEVITICUS 13:51-52; 14:34-45; LUKE 10:38-42)

100 Fold: The Deeper Story

> 14 "For He is our peace who hath made both one, and hath broken down the middle wall of partition between us;
> 15 Having abolished in His flesh the enmity, even the law of commandments contained in ordinances; for to make in Himself of twain one new man, so making peace;
> 16 And that he might reconcile both unto God in one body by the cross, having slain the enmity thereby;"
>
> (Eph. 2:14)

THIS PASSAGE IS BEAUTIFUL ON SO MANY LEVELS of understanding! But for the purposes of our parable, we can see that in Him we find **all** satisfaction to our every need whether it's redeeming a relationship between people or nations, or just in our own territory of the soul. He breaks down the walls and replaces our distortions with peace, fills our shattered fragments with peace. It is possible to live in the knowledge and trust that He will fulfill our deferred hope with peace, even while we are still waiting for the manifestation of the tree of life. This is because in the 100 Fold**, He** is our Tree of Life. "**He** is all, and in all" and our faith is in **Him**.

Take some time to meditate on these things, to acknowledge Him and remember His many graces toward you. Appreciate Him.

(Eph 2:14; Col.3:11)

The Twelfth Wall

The Loss of Ground & an Unlikely Teacher

SATISFIED WITH OUR SUCCESS FROM THE PREVIous adventure, we sat on the edge of the plateau overlooking the east valley from wince we had come. This satisfaction grew from the inside out, like an unstoppable cancer of thought. Cancer like, "Look how far you've come. Most people don't pay the price to achieve such heights." The temptation to become impressed with myself for this success was intense. The thoughts just kept coming. With each thought that came, Donkey's head seemed to inflate like a hot air balloon. Unicorn sat on the edge, focusing his attention on the Heavenly Realm. His face glowed with the delight of success that was given by The One. Had I followed Unicorn's lead and kept my eyes fixed on the Giver of all Good I would have noticed the interloper standing behind me, hovering over my head. He had snuck up from behind while I was basking in the pleasure of success. Knowing that these strong thoughts were full of self-aggrandizement, I spoke to the enemy I called "pride, spiritual pride." It is the greatest danger to a soul, for it raises itself above the knowledge of God. Because this was so blatant and arrogant, I came down from the inflated thoughts and began to follow the Unicorn's lead. My words of rebuke in the name of Jesus caused the interloper to fly backwards off the cliff. Donkey's head began to regain its intended size as the Giver of All Good was acknowledged for all of our successes. This infuriated the interloper! He brought back four more interlopers, making five altogether, and they were mean! Donkey was assaulted in every possible way. But the hardest hit was to his heart, when news of his beloved child's misfortune met his ears. We doubled over from an invisible punch to the belly and wailed in a grief so overpowering that the interloper called pain made full entrance. We collapsed on the plateau's smooth floor, full of emotional pain and sorrow. Then the final blow was dealt, resulting in a broken heart. Resignation arose and pushed us off the plateau of success, tumbling far, far down past all of the walls we had already overcome. The thought of having to ascend all over again brought a great depression with it. Considering the labor that was required to ascend the first time brought discouragement to a new epic low.

Later I was told that many travelers never come out from this treacherous domain. This is because they have known the high places of the Heavenly One and are very aware of the great distance they have fallen. Disillusioned by life's painful experiences they faint from the onslaught of pain and a broken heart who can bear. Their heart is broken from the loss of communion with the Lover of their soul. Our Creator calls out, "Will you still love Me?" "Will you still follow Me?" My answer is "Yes, but I have not the strength."

Lifting my face from the dirt, I looked to see where we had landed. It was the most barren wilderness known to man. Not one plant was in sight. No water was to be found except the tears I cried. I expected to find Donkey battered and bruised from the assault. But, no. He just laid there in defeat, too exhausted to move. With further inspection, an internal frightening picture appeared. It was

Darling, battered and bruised. These were bruises no one else could see. Pain had a friend called Accuser, Accuser of the brethren. Each thought delivered by Accuser brought forth intense pain and internal bleeding, which made Donkey very weak. All desire left me. All hope left.

Resignation stood over me, feeding me all the reasons I should just stay down in the dirt and give up. I listened. I stayed down in that acidic dirt called pain; for I was convinced I was to blame for the suffering of another. I learned that if an enemy can't bring you down by attacking *you*, he will attack those whom you love.

Accuser sent out a steady flood of thought which formed a significant wall. I believed every word. And every word caused a flood of tears to flow from Donkey's eyes. Watered by the steady flow of tears, the acidic dirt became a pool of mud. Moving at all was almost impossible under the weight. We laid there for a very long time, paralyzed in pain.

Unicorn seemed to have disappeared. I called and called to Him, but he must not have heard, for He never showed His face. I kept my eyes on Donkey, since at times Unicorn took his place, but not this time. Inside the Donkey, I was still resigned.

I laid down and waited for the redemption to be performed by the Heavenly One. This seemed holy to me, for I had not the strength to even contend with daily requirements of food. If not for Donkey, I would not have consumed food nor drink. I had not the power to save myself. Something prevented me from the desire to live life. I just wanted to die, to go home where the Unicorn resides. So I waited. Then suddenly I realized that Donkey had **kept** me alive. So I sat up inside that beast of burden and began to reprimand him.

"How dare you force me to live when I am so hurt? How dare you take another breath! I just want to die!"

I hadn't expected an answer from him. He was so docile, that beast of burden. He sat up and began to speak. "I have painful varicose veins in my legs because you, Darling, have stagnant blood!"

Astonished, I asked, "Why do I have stagnant blood?"

"You have not forgiven yourself for many things, including the fall."

"Well…how does that make my blood stagnant?"

"Self-righteousness."

I knew just what he meant. This self-righteousness

of expecting perfection of myself is a critical flaw, which serves to stagnate communion with the Lover of my Soul. No wonder His voice is rarely heard in my land these days! Oh, how I long to hear His voice as in days before this wilderness. I chose Adam's blood over the blood of the Lamb; self-righteousness over His righteousness; guilt instead of love; legalism instead of Grace. I was right to judge my actions, but solely to repent. I needed a spiritual blood transfusion to heal my condition! This is as simple as a change of mind!

Right then, I forgave myself for the long list I had held. I was very surprised that I even *had* a list, since forgiveness is a foundational teaching from long ago. My mood was immediately lifted and his veins were immediately healed. I wondered what else Donkey might know. Then I wondered what other pain I caused *him* to suffer. So I asked,

"What other pain do you have because of me?"

I waited a couple of minutes. Still no reply. I did notice, however, an uncomfortable feeling. It was a type of numbness I hadn't noticed before. Donkey still said nothing, though. So I let it go. Even still, I felt there was peace between us, though a secret still remained. I felt remorse for not having greater love for the Donkey all along. I regretted not getting to know him sooner.

Still in this contemplative mood, and still stuck in the mud, my thoughts wandered to Unicorn. I miss Him so. Intuitively these thoughts arose, "Your greatest danger is to rise up and curse God, blaming Him for your failure. Even thoughts of doing so wound your soul. For you are keenly aware of His great love, remembering the days of basking and bathing in His Presence, in His Love. Furthermore, you fervently love Him! Therefore, guilt is another strong contender for the possession of your soul. Unhealed guilt is the greatest separator from the Holy One, since it refuses to receive the unifying love of God, through the blood of our Savior. The end result is death in this wilderness."

Oh, where is my Great Deliverer! If only we could see Him. We might have more comfort and trust. But perhaps this was the very point of the whole matter. What trust is required if all is known and seen? No. Faith is developed in the not knowing, not-seeing. "Faith is the substance of things hoped for, the evidence of things not seen."(Heb. 11:1) When the soul is without understanding, it is forced to walk by faith, not by sight.

It was nighttime in the wilderness of my darling soul.

The next day, still burdened in the miry mud of pain who had brought another interloper called depression, a hummingbird came and hovered in front of our face. Donkey turned away, fearing that the little hummer's heart would fail to beat if it felt the depth of our pain. But the Little One persisted. Her heart did not fear for herself. She moved every direction we looked. By example of her flight pattern, she showed us how *she* overcame *her* pain.

Her flight seemed erratic and random. There was no fluid flight like other birds. First she telescoped straight up. Then she plummeted down in a 45-degree angle, barely missing a wrought iron fence. Watching her was like watching the ball in a pinball machine. There seemed to be neither rhyme nor reason to her flight. She kept returning to our face, peering deeply into our eyes as if to see whether we understood the process she was showing in her flight pattern. Several repetitions later, we caught on!

First she telescoped up, drawing our eyes to the sky. For us, this would be to focus on Him, the Lover of our soul.

Then she appeared to fall down. However, it turned out that she wasn't falling, but was chasing a bug to devour it. For us, this would be like chasing an interloper and overcoming it. The next bug might be over to the left and slightly above. So she would bolt in that direction and overcome that bug. Even she, as tiny and frail as she was, could overpower her prey and live another day. Again and again she would conquer a bug then return to her hover around her tree. She was territorial and guarding her nest.

Her flight wasn't random as it appeared. It was spontaneous and strategic, like points on a map. It means that we are to respond in the moment, being alert to the "bugs," the interloper lies. Then comes the strategy…crush the interloper with our words. Even as frail as we are, we can overcome our enemy, by speaking the great Word of the Heavenly One who tells us the Truth of who we really are. Then guard, with all diligence, the territory we have taken within our soul.

She came back to gaze into our eyes. This is what we must do with our heavenly father, even if we can't see Him, hear Him, or feel Him. We must return to His presence again and again, until we are filled with strength for the next conquering of the "bugs" in our life. This is how to overcome. Don't look at how far you've fallen. Only remember the Lover of your soul and how much He loves you.

Upon understanding, we were filled with love for the Little One who persisted with us until we could understand. As quickly as she had come, she left. Grateful as we were, we wondered why the Unicorn had not come to our rescue. This was something I would not understand for a very long time. I was tempted to distrust Unicorn, but I conquered that accusing interloper before he came in! Thereafter, it was an easy temptation to overcome. Nonetheless, Donkey and I agreed and moved as one unit. We stood up! This was an enormous feat, for the fall had severely misaligned Donkey's entire skeletal form. Nearly every joint was out of place. That nasty interloper of pain not only shoved him off the cliff, but also thrust itself into every joint. Our stand was short lived. Donkey collapsed in the miry mud only a little deeper still. This is because discouragement brought depression to the forefront. They spoke the same words: "You are a mess! Nothing can help you and you have disappointed the Holy One! He only helps those who help themselves."

Fraught with discouragement, I lifted my internal eyes to the Lord. "If I can't outside stand up, I can at least inside look up!" A song suddenly came to mind. "I lift my eyes to the hills. From where does my help come? My help it comes from the Lord, who made heaven and earth."

Looking around from this higher perspective was the endless view of the barren wilderness. Discouraging, indeed. This wilderness was unlike all others. The interlopers seemed familiar but the walls they built were much loftier. Limping along, Donkey and I discussed this. However we only had questions without answers. Donkey scratched his forehead, which was now filled with consternation. Just then, I remembered the Little One and the beauty of her love. This remembrance gave us just enough encouragement to continue. As always, the aching in my heart for the Unicorn continued. I felt I had disappointed Him, but I knew it was only myself who was surprised by the fall.

Together, Donkey and I agreed to apply the steps of flight taught to us by the Little One, a process we would repeat over and over again. For all of the walls we had already overcome had to be conquered once again, only this time with the aching of the

Donkey's joints which made him limp and slowed us down. The other hindrances included much more difficult terrain and the absence of the Unicorn's visual and verbal direction. Nonetheless, we walked. And we overcame many, many walls. Every morning we rose again and looked up to the Holy One then fought the interlopers as they appeared, just as the Little One had taught us in her flight. Depression and discouragement showed up every day. But we repeated the Little One's process.

We learned that in a deep wilderness, the Holy One sends a messenger to show the way out. This prevents spiritual pride. Furthermore, the interlopers only appeared to be giants. In the end, they appeared as they truly are, as small as the Little One's bugs!

Out of the blue, Donkey moved without consulting me. So I just let him lead. We couldn't find Unicorn in any of the ways previously learned. So, what could it hurt?

After a long time, we came to a cave in the ground, which had a cap securely covering its depth. We had been making our way through this unpaved wilderness, called Never Mind Trail, but it continued for hundreds and hundreds of miles, returning no fruit and no hope of a route out. So we sat down and pondered removing the cap. This treacherous domain had many secret chambers and many mysteries. The path we had been making seemed to bring us to a weakened state of mind. I felt woozy and confused. Donkey was weary and in pain. I despised seeing him in pain from that terrible fall. For he was the most faithful creature I had ever known. Even though I had not always appreciated him, I came to love and depend on him in many ways, especially in this wilderness when Unicorn could not be found. He rarely complained unless I chose to eat something that disagreed with him. His unspoken wisdom had helped me once I noticed and learned his quiet language. Even now he is quiet unless I am feeling sorrow or pain. He seems to mirror my feelings. The tremendous pain I felt from that massive fall, he seemed to express in his uneven gait. He is in distress and this distresses me.

All of this distress has made us very sleepy. We are frustrated and don't know the way to go. We've been sleepy since the fall, as a matter of fact. So we agreed to take a nap. Resting my head on the cap of the cave, along the side of Never Mind Trail. We quickly slipped into slumber.

(PROV. 13:15; PS 51:17; HEB. 11:1; PS 121:1)

Between the Walls

Disjointed in a Dark Night

AFTER THE APPARENT LOSS OF GROUND, THE soul's highest perspective was of an endless barren wilderness. This view, however, was its own perspective, not His Heavenly view. It was a view of discouragement and distorted ideas about the fall and what it meant.

The fall brought about by spiritual pride and lengthened by the issue of blood, legalism, took them on an almost endless path of confusion and weakness of mind. The thoughts of God are higher than man's thoughts. Trying to figure out what the fall was all about just brought consternation not peace. This condition is known as a Dark Night of the Soul, as recorded revelation through St. John of the Cross, 1542-1591.

A Dark Night of Soul is when understanding is dark, meaning there is no understanding of the mind, will and emotions. The gifts and workings of the spirit of God within the believer seem to be gone and the worst aspect is that God has seemed to remove Himself from the soul in all of the ways it is used to knowing Him. This is devastating to the soul and brings on a spiritual depression, not due to backsliding or sin. Rather, this action of God is bringing forth a progression of maturity in the soul. The soul is being darkened for a season to train it to trust and follow the leading of the Holy Spirit within instead of filtering everything through reason, which can become out of balance in the overall picture. This is a very frightening section of the path on the way to integration. The soul feels out of touch even with its Maker Who has hidden Himself. "How long will you, O Lord? Wilt thou forget me forever? How long wilt thou hide thy face from me? How long will I take counsel in my soul, having sorrow in my heart all the day?" Ps. 13:1-2 (NAS) In short, the soul feels lost and abandoned by God.

Outwardly, the person seems depressed, directionless, confused about life. The Lord permits many misunderstandings by others and increases their harsh judgments toward them. Friends and family retreat, striking at the souls' deep desire to be understood, accepted and loved. But the Lover of the Soul, Himself, knows the deepest need of each unique soul...to know God in every part of our being. Phil.3:10 "That I may know Him and the power of His resurrection and the fellowship of His sufferings, being conformed to His death." This is the cry of the soul who loves Him. So, He is faithful to answer our cry. John 14 tells us this is possible and is indeed God's desire, too.

The distorted view of the fall will be rectified through this Dark Night as the soul learns to live by faith in a deeper measure. It will come to understand that it was being deepened, not beaten; that it was a dive into the deep, not a fall into the abyss; it was drawing nearer God, not being cast away. It was a gathering of pieces and a rewiring of neurons. But the needful process in our story required the mind to be confounded and in a weakened state so that the spirit could rise to its proper status as leader in the trio's hierarchy, spirit, soul and body.

During this night of soul, the body and its quiet voice is brought to the forefront to both receive healing and to facilitate healing of the soul. The story speaks of physical distress and being "out of joint." When something is out of joint, it experiences weakness and inability to function at full capacity, if at all. So we see in the story, how the Holy Spirit (Unicorn) is uniting the soul (Darling) and body (Donkey) to a higher level of unity than previously experienced.

Joint=to separate, divide; spread or separate oneself (Strong's #6504), used in Ps. 22:14 during our Lord's crucifixion,

> *"I am poured out like water,*
> *And all my bones are **out of joint**;*
> *My heart is like wax;*
> *It is melted within me." (NAS)*

In it's first usage, Gen. 32:25 (Strong's #3363), it means "to sever oneself or to be dislocated; figuratively, to abandon; to impale (and thus allow to drop to pieces by rotting): -be alienated, depart, be out of joint."

So, to be out of joint means to have separated or severed one's self, rendering the self, which is the soul, in pieces, being alienated from your true essence (bone, i.e., "Bone of my bone").

Many people who have suffered childhood sexual abuse have seen themselves by vision or dream, shattered or in pieces. Albeit, abuse of any kind is not your fault! It was something that happened to you. Nonetheless, the true self is abandoned; the one whom God so loves and gave His only begotten son for, so you could have life!

In our story, the Donkey had slipped down from the Plateau of Success, having heard a traumatic report about a loved one. Hearing, seeing or feeling a trauma, can bring on dissociation. Sometimes our progress tends to be like a jagged graph of a woman bearing a child. As labor progresses through the transition phase the graph shows the forward then receding progress of the child's delivery. This can be very discouraging! But it isn't a loss of ground. It can be seen as a resting moment while giving birth. Sometimes this backward step may be due to the many shattered pieces being separate and unable to communicate with each other. The Truth that set one piece free has not been communicated to one still unintegrated. I call this emotional neuropathy. Just like physical neuropathy where the damaged nerves in part of the body cannot communicate with the foot, for example, so the foot doesn't know to feel the cold floor beneath it. Hence, it is numb. One may remember a trauma, but can't feel compassion for oneself and is stuck in only knowing about it. So, you may be emotionally numb from the neck down, or just a certain area of your body may be numb. This is where the beauty of your body's memory will be helpful to understand and heal yourself.

Body Recognition Exercise 1
Close your eyes and do a "body scan" starting with your head. Internally visualize each part of your body and notice if there is pain, numbness, tingling, burning or any sensation in each part. If there is, ask, "Why are you _____? Enter in the blank the sensation your body has. Then listen. Many times our body remembers things we've forgotten and it needs to be healed. Visions sometimes occur with this exercise. Just be open to letting the Holy Spirit be in control.

Body Recognition Exercise 2
On a positive note, you can close your eyes, to avoid distractions, and think of one of your favorite things to do. Notice the feeling in your chest, stomach... did you crack a smile? This exercise may

be useful in discovering ways to self-sooth or to finding your right path in life.

The point is that you can know yourself better by "listening" to your body's quiet language. Experts in soma (body) research say that the body never forgets and it never lies.

(Ps 13:1,2; Phil. 3:10; John 14; Ps 22:14 NAS)

100 Fold: The Deeper Story

THE FOLLOWING IS AN EXCERPT FROM A POEM written by St. John of the Cross, who lived from 1542-1591.

TRANSCENDING ALL KNOWLEDGE

*I entered unknowing,
and there remained unknowing
transcending all knowledge.*

*I entered into unknowing yet, when I saw myself there,
without knowing where I was,
I understood great things.*

*I will not say what I felt
for I remained in unknowing
transcending all knowledge.*

That perfect knowledge was of peace and holiness
held in profound solitude;

It was something so secret
that I was left stammering,
transcending all knowledge.

I was so 'whelmed, so absorbed and withdrawn
that my senses were left deprived
of all their sensing.

And my spirit was given an understanding,
while not understanding
transcending all knowledge.

He who truly arrives there cuts free from himself;
All that he knew before
now seems worthless,

And his knowledge so soars
that he is left unknowing,
transcending all knowledge.

The higher he ascends the less he understands
because the cloud is dark,
which lit up the night;

*whoever knows this
remains always in unknowing,
transcending all knowledge.*

*This knowledge in unknowing is so overwhelming
that the wise men disputing
can never overthrow it,*

*for their knowledge does not reach
to the understanding of not understanding,
transcending all knowledge.*

*And this supreme knowledge is so exalted
that no power of man
or learning can grasp it;*

*He who masters himself
will, with knowledge in unknowing,
always be transcending.*

*And if you should want to hear,
this highest knowledge lies, in the loftiest sense
of the essence of God;*

*This is a work of His mercy,
to leave one without understanding,
transcending all knowledge.*

This is a major turning point in the journey of the darling soul. Never Mind Trail has led her to deeper knowledge, which is in the Spirit. The soul is to play the supporting role, second place, with the Spirit in the leading role. To reverse the roles is to usurp the authority of God on His throne in the innermost chamber of you, His temple.

So, this unknowing that St John speaks of is a graduation into the 100 fold experience of God's inner presence with the soul. It is a confusing time. In this process the Spirit takes back its' rightful authority and a void is created in the soul (mind, will and emotions). As in Genesis, it is a beginning. Darkness of understanding is the souls' bread, day and night, and this is distressing to it. For a time, the soul feels deserted since all of its' ways and methods no longer seem to work. Every path it takes to commune with the Father seems to render nothingness in the way of communion. The giftings of the Spirit seem to be on leave. The soul thinks it did something wrong but can't figure out what. So it repents, nonetheless. Endless repenting produces no better communion and the soul tires of its' efforts. Finally!

The soul begins to rest in the workings of the

Spirit. As it does, communion with the Father increases and the spiritual giftings resurface with an increase in power. "And God said, Let there be light: and there was light. And God saw the light, that it was good: and God divided the light from the darkness. And God called the light Day, and the darkness he call Night." This, indeed, is a dark night for the soul, but as it gives up all of its' strivings, the Lord brings light, for He is the Light of the world.

When the soul meddles in the workings of the Spirit we have what is called mixture. It's like having a high quality of wine from the best vineyard and adding water! This process of the dark night births a new day in the life of the soul and may take months to years of the Spirit hovering over the deep. Some souls can bear a constant working without breaks. Other dear souls require times of light between the darkness, so as to prevent damage to its' tender make-up. Whichever is the case for you, dear reader, don't be dismayed. Our Father knows you better than you know yourself. And His love and care of you is perfect!

(JOB 13:20; PS. 27:9; 69:17; 102:2; 143:7; GEN. 1:1-5)

The Thirteenth Wall

Isolated in Fragmented Memories

As we slept, I began to dream of the Unicorn. A slender rain fell from the heavenlies indicating another cleansing was soon to come. Searching the dreamy tropical terrain, the Unicorn was nowhere to be found. In my dream I began to weep out of desperation. To be whole, to be unified seemed so beyond my reach. I knew Unicorn could show me the way but I had run out of strength to search for him. His voice could no longer be heard for I was consumed with the sound of my own thoughts and sorrows.

In the dream I found myself in the basement of my house. A man with a spear was stalking me. I tried to call for help, but could not find my voice. Running upstairs and past a doorway, I saw a young maiden chained and hemorrhaging from her wounds. She had a cone of shame around her neck and her head hung toward the ground. Her hair hung over her face such that I could not see her. When she looked up at me, I screamed for she had the eyes of the Unicorn, but in fact, she was Me, Darling!

Lightening and a clap of thunder shook me from my dream. I huddled beneath some leaves of a nearby fig tree, shaking from fear. The dream frightened me to the core. Suddenly I caught a glimpse of Unicorn. Unbeknownst to me, he had been following close behind for quite some time. Acknowledging that he had been seen, he bounded to my side. "Where were you?" I cried. "We were attacked by a band of interlopers and I could not find you! Why didn't you help me?" Looking into his soft, compassionate eyes, my fear dissolved and I broke-down in tears. Pulling me close, he said he had covered my backside, for he is my rear guard. "The interloper who's whisperings had caused Donkey's head to swell with pride had returned to finish you off. But," he said, "I intervened and protected you from an attack you would not have recovered from. I will never leave you, nor forsake you." "Now, about that cap, I want to remove the cap of the cave within you and heal what is inside."

I drew back in fear, uncontrollably hyperventilating. Donkey and I felt sick and I wanted to say "No," but I had never said that word to Unicorn, for I trusted Him. Everything He ever did had been for my benefit and out of pure love. So I acquiesced.

He began running counter clockwise around the perimeter of the cap, loosening its seal. This counter clockwise swirl began to awaken fragments of a memory buried within the cave of myself. In the pale rain, these fragments looked reflective, alive, each one possessing a piece of my life I could not remember. Some of the fragments seemed familiar but incoherent. And some reflected pain of various kinds. They began to gather like fragments of a stained glass window, but dark, opaque. Donkey shook uncontrollably, curling into a fetal position. My emotions stirred to the highest degree of fear so I reached for that ancient tool of emotional control…numbness to separate me from the pain. Doing this caused me to isolate, to separate from Donkey and Unicorn. This numbness was indeed a wall and a symptom of those secret caverns spoken of in the vast wilderness.

In the midst of my turmoil I heard Unicorn's

soft voice say "I have loved you with an everlasting love. Trust me once again." Knowing He was with me was all I needed. For He had so smartly proven His faithfulness, gentleness and love toward me through all the previous adventures, such that I found no justification distrusting Him. So I released my grip upon my defensive tool, emotional numbness (dissociation) and let myself feel the labor pains of birthing myself, a person I hardly knew.

At this very moment, a heavenly shofar blasted its' mournful call. With a synchronous gasp, Donkey and I hyperventilated. Some of the fragments looked like enemies surrounding me. Some began to scatter and fall away. Where they went, I could not tell. But the remaining fragments wouldn't budge from their positions, creating a wall between the Unicorn, the Donkey and me. I could see that the Unicorn wasn't isolated, but *I* was the one shut out, alone. This numbness is the isolated pain I stored in Donkey because I wasn't ready to know what the fragments were all about, fragments that were buried beneath the cap of the cave, things I wanted to forget.

Simultaneously we dropped to the ground,

howling like a wolf caught in the iron jaws of a poacher's trap. I howled out a sorrowful repentance for hiding the pain, for numbing out. Donkey howled out pain that the self-imposing interloper had inflicted upon us in our youth. This had shattered our being and kept us from integrating, from operating as one unit, from being made whole in the Holy One.

My understanding was of necessity blinded for the duration of our release. Body and soul moved in unison, expelling fright-filled traumas from our midst. Emotions quieted. Donkey lay limp, but in perfect alignment. His body was worn out as one who has labored for years to carry a load too heavy for his frame, a load he was never intended to bear alone.

Light beams filtered into the bottom of the cave, the very depth of my being, the basement of my being. The rain had ceased. A wispy rainbow caressed the sky. The once vast wilderness of nothingness had been transformed into the dewy tropical paradise it was intended to be.

Looking up was a mosaic window that had been so dark and frightening. All of the shattered pieces of our essence had been soldered together, forming one essence, one whole. It was a stained glass window in the form of a beautiful woman. It was the maiden I had seen in my dream! No longer chained, I could now move without pain. No longer emotionally numb; no more shame! I could see through the window, the window of Heaven. My eyes are now clear. Unicorn, Donkey and Me had integrated, spirit, body and soul, by way of facing our pain. The Holy One's Presence facilitated our ingathering from the four corners of our earth. All of our parts became One. I had the sensation of my shoulders becoming internally full, filled out, nothing missing! I AM WHOLE! YESHUA HEALS! And I dwell between His shoulders as Benjamin dwelt between His shoulders, devouring the prey that sought to devour me, and in the evening of my life, I shall divide the spoils, the riches of wisdom from my journey to wholeness in Him!

Our many shattered pieces which preserved our life at one time, must be acknowledged, healed and integrated or released. Then we are made whole by the only One who can tell us who we truly are.

Thus, the shattered fragments of our true essence are integrated and our bones become rightly fitted together at the time of our personal, mystical resurrection.

> *Oh, Father, Lover of my soul! Thank-you for integrating my whole being and restoring the very precious, God given essence of my personality, restoring strength, hope, will, identity and solid integrity in the One who created me, Christ Jesus! To restore, repair or recreate all that was damaged through traumas and abuse of every kind; to be rightly connected, joined together - as each bone in my body carries my essence in Your DNA and is vital to the very substance of my individual being. May I be rightly fitted together in the Body of Christ May I only submit in complete surrender only unto You, the Lover of my soul!*

A banqueting table appeared, full with guests who had interceded on my behalf. Beautiful music played in the background songs I had never heard. A band, however, was not present. The music emanated from my own heart, that beautiful maiden. She...I had found my voice! Soon the guests played forth the instrument within their hearts, too. A more beautiful sound has never been heard, except of course, the seraphim's alluring chant of "Holy, Holy, Holy," which is in the hearts of all His royal people.

There I was, on the plateau of joy and feasting. No longer three parts seen separately, acting separately, but one, integrated maiden. Isolation is no longer welcomed here.

And the Spirit said, "Where are your enemies?" reminding me of the woman caught in adultery. Yeshua effortlessly and without violence saved her in a moment. I realized that the adulteress had been me, hiding behind so many walls of lovers, eating the bread at so many foreign tables, keeping me away from Him, the Lover of my soul.

(Is. 52:12; Heb. 13:5; Is. 6:3)

Between the Walls

Re-Member: The Method

FRAGMENTED MEMORIES OFTEN TIMES SURFACE as a dream, revealing the deepest trauma within the soul. Thus exposing the abuse in symbolic terms, which is all that her fragmented essence can endure in her disjointed condition. Since she is now awakened to the truth of her past suffering, she can run into the Lord as a Strong Tower and pour out her many emotions. Holy Spirit direction is crucial. He leads the soul into all truth. And now by His truth, she is being set free. "For the Lord is good and His love endures forever!"

Weeping at His feet facilitates the release of this long forgotten trauma. Fragments of her soul are still captive surface from the dark and take their rightful place in her personality, like a jigsaw puzzle. Now understanding comes to her. She can make sense of her past and some unusual behaviors, emotions and decisions she has made. Compassion for herself rises and judgment falls away. So, too, every voice that accused her is silenced.

In your own life, consider the traumas that you've lived through and how they've shaped your life. How have they created pain, formed your beliefs about life, relationships, the world, God? As you consider these things allow all emotions to surface without judgment. Cry out to God if you are mad at Him. Just say it! He already knows it, anyway. Total honesty with Him is the best path to wholeness and healing. Allow full release of your feelings before God.

A sample prayer, or as I like to say, a talk with the God Who loves you might look like this:

> *Father, I am spent! I am frustrated and angry! I don't know why this trauma had to happen, why my life has been so painful, chaotic, (fill-in-the-blank). My heart is broken and I know you are my only hope! Please heal my brokenness, my spirit, soul and body. I repent for all sin in my life and I thank-you that when I call, You hear me and answer me in Your wisdom and timing. You have saved me!*

I give you all of my emotions and I acknowledge that they in themselves are not evil, but alert me to pay attention to my soul. My emotions are indicators that something inside of me may need tending to. If it is contrary to peace and love, I pray for healing, for we are led forth by the peace of the Holy Spirit and you said, Great peace have they which love thy law: and nothing shall offend them." Ps. 119:165. I repent and seek you for healing whatever is inside of me that doesn't love you! And I forgive You for the things You didn't do the way I wanted and when I wanted You to do them. I love You! In Jesus' name, Amen.

What follows is a method to integration. Another highly effective method is the use of EMDR's discovered by Francine Shapiro. Her book, *Getting Past Your Past* is a self-help book on how to perform EMDR on yourself. It is listed in the back of this book. Please start with the following method so that your spiritual foundation is laid. Any tool you use after this will be far more effective.

Re-Member: The Method

Step 1: Address our Father in Heaven
Father, Adonai, Daddy, Abba, Papa, whatever your favorite address is for Him, call upon Him and thank Him for who He is and for His everlasting love for you, grace and mercy.

Step 2: Repent
Re = "again"; Pent = from, *"poena,"* meaning, punishment (Webster's)

So, the conscience suffers self "punishment" until it comes clean with the truth of it's actions, thoughts and intentions. Of coarse there is nothing hidden from the eyes of the Lord. He knows everything, so it behooves us to keep secrets from Him! It only serves to torment ourselves! So come clean quickly with Him and yourself.

Step 3: Forgive
To give up, or away. (Webster's)

"I give up my offense toward _____ and I cancel the debt he/she owes me."

Step 4: Interlopers Cast Off
Interlopers in this story refer to other spirits outside of the Holy Spirit, such as fear, trauma, pain, depression, murder, self-pity, discouragement, etc.

Step 5: Arms of Jesus Emotional Healing
Allow your imagination to picture Jesus, crawl up into His arms and let yourself be nurtured. Soak in His Presence. You can use worship music, musical instruments, sing or dance to aid in this.

Step 6: Spiritual Blood Transfusion
Receive for yourself, again, the very DNA of Jesus. Exchange Adam's bloodline for that of Jesus' Bloodline. Repent for the sins of your ancestor's all the way back to Adam.

Step 7: Re-Member (Integrate)
Receive back every part of yourself that has been separated, cut-off, isolated, numbed-out, silenced or otherwise cast out or shattered.

Step 8: Return

From Latin word *retornare*—Re = again; *tornare* = to turn back (Webster's)

Go back to our Father and love Him, thank Him for healing you!

Sample Prayer

Abba Father, I love You! My soul thirsts for You and I am hungry for your presence. Thank-you, for being with me (even if He feels distant, He is always there with you). And I thank-you, for loving me and being gracious to me.

Father, I have noticed this _____ about myself and I know it has separated me from You (sin) in my soul. I want You to own me in every part of myself, Your mansion. Please forgive me for my sins against You as I choose, by an act of my will, to forgive _____ for his/her (<u>sins</u>) against me. I cancel the debt I feel he/she owes me. He/she owes me nothing. I repent, also, for the iniquity of my ancestors and their sinful bloodline, all the way back to Adam. Thank-you, Father for Your forgiveness!

I give up the pain, chaos and trauma this caused me, and in Jesus' name, I cast them out of my presence and send them to the feet of Jesus. I take authority according to Luke 9:1, over the spirit of (list the spirits which the Holy Spirit brings to your mind) and I command it to leave me and go to the feet of Jesus, never to return to me again. I close all connections I had with those spirits and seal myself with the Blood of Jesus that cleanses me from all sin and heals my brokenness.

Father, I rest in Your Presence, now, and I ask every part of me that You created to remember who You created them to be. That is, WHOLE! So I command every part of me to be joined with my very essence. I welcome every part, shattered piece, cast-off piece, every forgotten piece of my soul to reconnect and be one whole with me as I am whole in Him! I love you and thank-you for helping to protect me when I didn't know how to run into our Father as my strong defense and protector. You can be at peace, now, because we are one with Him. Soul, be healed! Body, be healed! Spirit, be healed!

Thank-you, Father! In Jesus' Beautiful Name, Amen

(John 14; John 17, especially vs. 11 "...that they may be one even as We are one." and vs. 21 "That they may all be one; even as Thou, Father, art in Me and I in Thee, that they also may be in Us;...")

*This process is offered on author's website as a workshop called Re-Membering

The Fourteenth Wall

Skin Is a Veil

FINALLY, THE TIME ARRIVED TO SET OUT TOWARD the Pinnacle of Re-Membering. Though the distance is short, the grade is steep and jagged. Endurance and focus are needed.

Surprised by my exuberance so early in the morning, I bounded uphill almost effortlessly. This is the evidence of the Unicorn's presence in the body, for the spirit of a man will sustain his infirmity, but a wounded spirit who can bear? I am peaceful within *and* feel the fullness of my body. No numbness remains and no separation, for Donkey and I are integrated...body and soul.

All of Unicorn's abilities are now my abilities, for we, also are in union of Spirit. Now is the time to use Unicorn's gift of buoyancy from the blessings of the Wall of Accusations. He can bound long distances, but with the sharp hairpin turns, the danger of over-shooting the path and falling one-thousand feet seemed immense.

I couldn't understand how to do it, since I continually miscalculated the jumps. A mysterious magnetic pull reeled me into the mountain path again and again. But I was not afraid of falling. For the Spirit had given me the understanding of my fall. Since I had hidden the pain of my abuse beneath the cap, the enemy had legal ground to attack. I had not trusted the Unicorn with my whole heart. Instead, I kept some control, emotional control, which kept me from feeling. I knew anger and fear, but not joy to the fullest. No other emotions seemed to work. Trust was continually reinforced by the hidden magnetic pull within the mountain core and his own heart.

Catastrophic failure was never really possible, though I didn't know that at the time. If I had, perhaps I wouldn't have feared.

Nonetheless, those walls were all so purposeful. For they not only removed my fears, numerous as they were, they also removed my belief in lack. I had believed that I was not enough, that somehow I was missing something, that I was hopelessly faulty.

Gleefully we leaped as one, again and again. And

I cried at the sense of safety, the profound protection in the midst of danger, mostly due to my own miscalculations, poor decisions and failure to flow in the unction of the Unicorn.

At this juncture, I sensed a wall like no other. It was the wall of my skin. Grounded but not. For in the spirit I could go out and return freely. For as I watched from within, I sprouted wings! I thought the magnetic pull would overcome the power of the wind in my wings, but it didn't.

In unison, the wings emerged and the magnet released its pull, as if this plan had been discussed prior.

However, I knew it was a working of the Spirit in the moment. The earthly Donkey merging completely with the Heavenly Unicorn and with me, the maiden, they, we flew to our hearts content, masterfully as if we had been created to soar.

Then with a sharp nose dive, reminiscent of the Little One, we pierced back through the atmospheric clouds, into the hollow womb of the mountain. It was like a volcano. No, it *was* a volcano, the very heart of the earth.

The wind gave way to the power of magnetic force within the mountain, within my heart.

Pressure of 5 G's, the fullness of grace, pulling me; I thought I would be separated from my skin, just as the unicorn had once sloughed off the donkey's coat. But that wasn't to be the case. The boundary of skin was to remain for now, until the holy day of His return. This is what the Unicorn referred to when at the 4th wall. He said that a promise had been made centuries ago, a promise to be fulfilled at the end of the age. He saw down through the ages the resurrection of our mortal bodies.

Upon seeing the very source of light in the depths I gasped in awe. What should have blinded me enlightened me. What should have devoured me strengthened me. Reminiscent of Moses' burning bush, it was the fire of God within the depths of the mountain giving, receiving and returning continuously with every breath.

Nervous resistance gave way to trusting peace. When I trusted, an infusion of fire whipped through my bones and remained. Most of the journey involved laboring to enter His rest, but this was like a gift I didn't have to open. It was all so passive! All I had to do was trust. "Only believe."

Fully abiding, I laid down in the midst of the Fire of Love. There shall my soul remain, hid in His

Presence always, until the time of the end when His everlasting promise will be fulfilled...the resurrection of the body made new in His image; the Pinnacle of Re-Membering!

(Prov. 18:14; Deut. 5:23, 24; Jer. 20:9 NIV; Lam 1:13 NAS; Heb. 3 & 4; 1Cor. 15-39-57)

Between the Walls

Abiding

Yeshua said, "Abide in Me; and I in you" John 15:4. To abide in any other spirit than the Holy Spirit is to be separate from Him, to commit adultery in a spiritual sense. To abide in Him is life, love, freedom, fruitfulness, safety, and companionship. Abide means to "stay (in a given state), relation or expectancy; continue, dwell, endure, be present, remain…" especially for those who have wandering minds or are prone to dissociation, *to be present* in each moment is the bottom line. Keep your thoughts on Him, acknowledging Him.

A good habit to develop is to make your first waking hour your God time. Read His word until you find something that inspires your heart. Sop right there. Re-read that phrase or section. Then close your eyes and meditate on what you just read. Let the peace of God permeate your whole being.

Breathe His breath of life. Stay in this state for as long as you can. This practice will grow longer in time and deeper in the Spirit the more you practice it. The more you practice, the longer you will remain in this state during every day activities until finally, it will be a constant state of being. This is abiding!

A very serious obstacle to abiding is unbelief. Hebrews chapters 3 and 4 are dedicated to this topic of entering into His rest, which is abiding. Read these chapters frequently.

Ps. 91 gives the benefits of dwelling in the Secret Place. Many believers claim Psalm 91 for their lives, but do not know how to dwell in the Secret Place, which is the only requirement for all of His benefits listed therein. Yeshua said to abide in Him, so it is a choice. It is a choice we have to keep making every day and in every moment, and in every situation. Therefore, Psalm 91 and all of its' benefits are dependent upon our choosing to abide in His Spirit, in His ways. Just remember that we live according to His grace, His unmerited favor. It is the intention of the heart that God watches.

Having come to this wall of skin, Darling is exhilarated! She runs and does not become weary.

She sprouts wings and flies in the Spirit, in union with Him. Her heart is fulfilled, not with the desire for insignificant things but with the true longing of her heart, which was for union with Him, the Lover of her soul, for He, Himself, is the Tree of Life! He is the mountain she climbed and His fire is deep within her bones. That fire has been there all along. It's what has driven her to continue on Never Mind Trail to finally come to the Pinnacle of Re-Membering who she is, re-turning to her Father, and remaining.

Scriptures for abiding:

(Ex. 19:4;Ps. 27:5; Ps. 31:20; Ps. 91; Is. 40:31; JOHN 14, 15, 16, 17; HEB. 3 & 4; 1JOHN 2)

DARK NIGHT OF THE SOUL
by St. John of the Cross

On a dark night, kindled in love with
yearnings-oh happy chance!
I went forth without being observed,
my house being now at rest.
In the happy night, in secret, when none saw me,
Nor I beheld aught, without light or guide,
save that which burned in my heart.
This light guided me more surely than the light of
noonday,
to the place where he (well I knew who!) was
awaiting me
A place where none appeared.
Oh, night that guided me, Oh, night more lovely
than the dawn,
Oh, night that joined Beloved with Lover,
Lover transformed in the Beloved!

Upon my flowery breast, kept wholly for Himself alone,

There He stayed sleeping, and I caressed Him,

And the fanning of the cedars made a breeze.

The breeze blew from the turret as I parted His locks;

with His gentle hand He wounded my neck

and caused all my senses to be suspended.

I remained, lost in oblivion; My face I reclined on the Beloved.

All ceased and I abandoned myself,

leaving my cares forgotten among the lilies.

Glossary

BONE in the original Hebrew language, 'etsem, means "strength; substance, bone, life (Strong's #6106); and, as "the skeleton of the body; hence self." Further study of the bones connects the word "denude," meaning to make bare, to strip; to divest of all covering; to make bare or naked." Finally! We are brought back to the bare self, naked as Adam in the Garden, striped down to the very essence of who we truly are without any internal walls or "fig leaves" to hide behind, isolating us from God. At this point there is nowhere to hide from the One with whom we have to do. Our Fathers great love has denuded us to the very bone and in the Spirit, we stand before Him in perfect innocence, nude and without shame, covered only by the Blood of Jesus, HIS RIGHTEOUSNESS.

BROKENHEARTED – STRONG'S #7665, "Shabar=to break in pieces; break in or down, rend violently, wreck, crush, quench; to break, rupture (fig); be maimed, crippled, be wrecked; to shatter, break." (Is. 61:1; Luke 4:18)

DARLING – See definition of "Me."

DISSOCIATE – to separate from fellowship

DISSOCIATION – a separation
1. the act of taking apart or dissociating; a state of disunion; separation.

2. in chemistry, the breaking up of a compound into simpler components.

3. in psychology, the process in which a group of mental activities breaks away from the main stream of consciousness and functions as a separate unit: an intensified dissociation can lead to multiple personality,

DONKEY – the body.
Many people are dissociated from their body, not listening to its wisdom, i.e., when it is full, to stop eating. Even with promiscuity, a person with sexual abuse will ignore, or simply be numb to physical touch in certain areas. Many emotions are felt in the traumatized body, but not felt psychologically or emotionally. Some people cannot put a label on an emotion except for the most obvious one, anger. But the body has many "tells" even when the

numbed-out person is oblivious. For example, the feet, or one foot pointed away from the person you are holding conversation with, tells that you want to get away or leave that conversation. The body never lies. Our soul may be sleeping, but the body functions continuously at a more primal level, or else our heart would stop beating and our lungs would stop breathing.

DOOR denotes a threshold into a new thing or understanding. Strong's #2374 in the Greek, a portal or entrance; the opening or the closure, literally or figuratively). See Genesis 4:7. The Hebrew root word means to open wide, break loose, to let go free.

DUST (Strong's #6083) is the earthen mortar our Maker uses to bond the collection of a shattered soul, forming the beautiful mosaic window of that soul's life made whole. Shattered pieces of the soul are uniquely colored with the experiences of an over-comer's life. Pain, betrayal, disappointment and personal failures are Masterfully healed then integrated into one beautiful, unified window. The Light of the Master then shines forth through the window, showing off the beauty of a soul made whole.

The lesson of the dust of death is that as we

submit ourselves to the fellowship of His sufferings and are conformed unto His death, (See Philippians 3:10) then the shattered pieces of our life are gathered together in our individual resurrection to form the window of our soul, which is the anointing on our life, intensified by the death of false selves and agendas contrary to the will of God. (Please see "Window")

DUST OF DEATH is exactly what it says regarding the physical body, "From dust to dust," Gen. 3:19. In regards to our story, though, if you can imagine being so low (emotionally, intellectually, spiritually, physically) that you cannot pick your head up out of the dust, this is the state of the soul in complete surrender during crucifixion. (Strong's #6083, clay, earth, ashes, dust, ground, mortar, powder, rubbish.) It is the dust of death with which our Maker solders together the shattered pieces of our soul. A beautiful stained glass window is the result. "Beauty for ashes!" (Isaiah 61:3)

EDEN – metaphorically, the place of God's throne in man.

EMOTIONS – an element of the soul and are indicators of our soul's level of health or sickness. If it is contrary to peace, pray for healing. We are "lead forth by peace" by the Holy Spirit. Ps. 119:165 "Great peace have they which love thy law: and nothing shall offend them." If you are offended, ask yourself what emotion is connected to the offence. Is it your pride, a critical or jealous spirit? Repent and seek Him to heal whatever is inside that doesn't love Him.

FRETTING LEPROSY is found in chapter 11.
Donkey, the body, is burdened down with many things. It is "the sin of worry; anxiety; carefulness; bitterness"

Luke 10:38-42 is an account of the sisters, Mary and Martha.

HAND – power and possession; a person's works or what one does in life: an open hand indicates letting go; a closed hand can mean ownership. Young babies have tightly closed hands, as if to say they are holding onto all that they can. At death, people's hands are open and letting go. Jesus said, "You must lose your life to gain it." So, as we are living on this earth, we must learn how to surrender our internal grasp, holding onto affections not ordained by Father God.
Psalm 22:16

16 "For dogs have compassed me: the assembly of

the wicked have inclosed me: they pierced my hands and my feet.

HEART (Strong's 3824; 3820). The heart is melted like wax. That is, the emotions the will and the intellect are soft, compliant and without struggle against the Father's will. This is a picture of total surrender from within, from the very depths...the bowels of a person. This is a reference to the deep and hidden passions, which drive all behavior. The passions are the motives and agendas of a person, whether known or unknown, conscious or unconscious. (See Brokenhearted)

HORN, (Strong's #7161), figuratively speaking, symbolizes power. When Abraham was called up to Mount Moriah to sacrifice his son, Isaac, "a ram was caught in the thicket by its horns" (Gen. 22:13). Its power was restrained, allowing Abraham to sacrifice the ram in place of his son. As we are led by Holy Spirit up to our own Mount Moriah to lay down a particular habit, emotion or idea, we restrain the power of our soul and submit to the Holy fire of God within His Presence to purify our soulish power (the power of will, the power of mind, the power of our emotions).

Horns are also found on the Ark of the Covenant

in the Tabernacle. To take hold of the horns of the altar was symbolic of taking hold of God's protection, being protected by the power of God (Ex. 21:14; I Kings 1:50). When we submit our will to His will, we are protected from the evil one who seeks to devour our soul.

IDOL – a replacement for God; anything a soul internally runs to for comfort, protection, safety. In a dissociated soul, it's an escape into a fragmented piece of the soul that may or may not have a demonic stronghold. It must be acknowledged that NOT ALL fragments hold demonic entities. According to Strong's Concordance, an idol is (Strong's #457), "good for nothing, by anal. vain or vanity; spec. an idol: -idol, no value, thing of naught It can be anything that you acknowledge above God, Himself, in any given circumstance; food, for example, exercise, another person, acts of seeking to find answers through divination, astrology or any such activities, pornography. Truly, we can make idols out of most anything or anyone or any activity.

INTEGRATE – (L. integratus, pp. of integrare, to make whole, renew, from integer, untouched, whole, entire.

1. to make whole or complete by adding or bringing together parts.

2. to put or bring (parts) together into a whole; to unify

3. to give or indicate the whole, sum, or total of

4. in mathematics, (a) to calculate the integral or integrals of (a function, equation, etc.); (b) to perform the process of integration upon.

INTEGRATION – n.
1. an integrating or being integrated.

2. in mathematics, the process of finding the quantity or function of which a given quantity or function is the derivative of differential: opposed to differentiation.

3. in psychoanalysis, the organization of various traits or tendencies into one harmonious personality.

INTEGRITY – n. (L. integritas, wholeness, soundness, from integer, untouched, whole, entire.)

1. the quality or state of being complete; wholeness, entireness; unbroken state.

2. the entire unimpaired state or quality of anything; perfect condition; soundness.

3. the quality or state of being of sound moral principle; uprightness, honesty, and sincerity.

INTEGER – n. (L. integer, untouched, whole, entire; in-priv., and tanger, to touch.)
1. anything complete in itself; entity; whole.

2. a whole number (e.g., 5,10,748, etc.): distinguished from fraction.

COMPLEX integer; the sum of a real and an imaginary integer.

INTERLOPERS are those who intrude, legally or illegally, into the life, spirit, soul or body of a person, inflicting one with a different personality or identity other than that given sovereignly by Father God.

JAWS can refer to a strong will, as His jaw is set like flint, in chapter 4. However, Ps. 22:15 is referring to His physical tongue cleaving to his natural jaws from sever dehydration.

JESUS – the English pronunciation of the Greek translation of YESHUA, which is the name of Jesus in Hebrew, His original name!

JOINT (Strong's #6504) means to separate, divide; spread or separate oneself; used in Ps. 22:14 during our Lord's crucifixion. In it's first usage, Gen. 32:25 (Strong's #3363) it means to sever oneself" or to be dislocated; fig. to abandon; to impale (and thus allow to drop to pieces by rotting): -be alienated, depart,...be out of joint." Compare with Prov. 25:19 ("Confidence in an unfaithful man in time of trouble is like a broken tooth, and a foot out of joint."), having to do with being made to slip (Strong's 4154).

LAND, see definition of "Me."

ME – the SOUL, DARLING, the mind, the will, the emotions, which make-up the personality. Ps. 22, the Messianic Psalm foreshadowing His crucifixion, refers to His soul as "my darling." Soul in Hebrew is Strong's #5315, nephesh, meaning a breathing creature; mind; heart, from Strong's #5314, meaning to breathe; to be breathed upon. In Greek, it is Strong's #5590...psuche (from which the English word psyche is derived). Closely related is the word heart; (Strong's#3820). In the Bible, the soul is referred to as "land," "territory," "nations. We are called to "possess the land," "subdue the nations," "to have dominion," "to tend the garden." On one level of understanding, these are all metaphors for a human being taking charge of himself/herself, disciplining the soul, having dominion over the soul and body (referred to as the earth in scripture). Nations can be likened to the souls' faculty of imagination, which can be used for pure or impure imaginings, dreams and goals.

NUMBERS
9 in the Hebrew alphabet is represented by the letter tet, which has the meaning of goodness (Genesis 1, "good" is used 7 times); physical manifestation (the creation, Genesis 1) and pregnancy, birth; the 9 fruit of the Spirit (love, joy peace, patience, kindness, goodness, gentleness, faithfulness & self-control, Galatians 5:22) and the 9 gifts of the Spirit (word of wisdom, word of knowledge, faith, healings, miracles, prophecy, discerning of spirits, diverse tongues, interpretation of tongues, I Corinthians 12:7-11). It is the number of Divine

judgment and the hour of prayer (Yeshua died in the 9th hour thus taking our judgment upon Himself). Nine is also used in the Bible to reference judgment. For example, on the 9th of Av (a summer month on God's original calendar), the first two Temples were destroyed.

14 – comprised of a 4 (in Hebrew, dalet=door) and a 10 (Hebrew, yod=hand). It is interesting to note that there are 14 bones in a person's fingers and thumb, representing the works of a person, the things one does. Passover is on Nissan 14 on the Hebrew calendar and represents deliverance from Egypt, symbolic of slavery; also passing over the Jordan River from Egypt to Canaan the Promised Land or from death to Life, which is in Christ Jesus, Messiah, Yeshua ha Meshiach. The perfect Passover Lamb was and is lived out in the life and death of our Savior and in our own lives, taking us from Adam's isolation (a form of dissociation) to unity in the Second Adam, Jesus.

The significance of 14, then, is that our works, the things we do in life must be brought into submission by the workings of the cross in our own lives.

According to Phil. 3:10, "That I may know Him and the power of His resurrection and the fellowship of His sufferings, being conformed unto His death."

We must identify with Him and His crucifixion, taking up our own cross and following Him to our own crucifixion. This crucifixion dismantles all false identities we have taken to be our own: those walls of beliefs or entities that keep us separated and alone within the confines of our soul and body.

SECRET PLACE is the Garden of your being, hidden from the eyes of men. It is that place where one meets with and abides with God. The secret place is EDEN, the place that Adam (mankind) was banished from and Jesus made the way for our return. The Blood Sacrifice of Jesus thus allows us back into the Garden where we can freely commune with our Maker. What makes this difficult for us are the many "walls" we hide behind. These are the many ways we have divorced ourselves from Him by hiding ourselves away in dissociations (self-protections) once used to shelter us from painful events. We, therefore, are on a mission to return to Him and His shelter, trusting in none-other. This Returning is the topic of the entire Bible!

A good place to begin is to pray this simple prayer:

Father, I only want to abide with You and none other. Please draw me, cause me to love You with my whole heart, soul, and body. In Jesus' name, Amen.

SIN, in short, is anything that separates a person from the presence God, whether it be beliefs, actions or habits.

SOUL, see definition of "Me."

UNICORN – In this little parable, the Spirit of God dwelling within the believer is symbolized by the Unicorn. It is that place, the secret place hidden from the natural eyes of man, where the soul longs to return to the full-time communion with its Creator.

The King James Version is the only version of the Bible that I've found "wild ox" translated as "unicorn" (Strong's #7214, a wild bull [from its conspicuousness] from #7213, ra'am, meaning to rise: -be lifted up). Unicorn, or its plural form, unicorns, is used nine times in the King James Version. Since the vision given to me contained a unicorn to depict the Holy Spirit within me, I chose to be true to the vision given.

Being that a wild ox (unicorn) is wild, untamable by man and is also a sacrificial animal, it is considered in this book to be a symbol of Jesus Christ, Yeshua ha Meshiach who made the ultimate blood sacrifice for all of mankind.

Folklore has it that a unicorn is wholly pure, shy, elusive and will only reveal itself to a virgin maiden, to whom he will peacefully rest his head upon her lap and commune with her in quiet repose. For people who have significant trauma in their past, Yeshua presents Himself with gentleness, love and acceptance. This is why the unicorn has soft, gentle lines and is not fiercely drawn until the soul can accept Him in His fierceness, which is used to rescue her from her assailants. He is the soul's teacher, usually teaching by example and always with love.

Unicorn, or its plural form, unicorns, is used nine times in the King James Version, the same number used for the 9 fruit of the Spirit (love, joy peace, patience, kindness, goodness, gentleness, faithfulness & self-control, Galatians 5:22) and the 9 gifts of the Spirit (word of wisdom, word of knowledge, faith, healings, miracles, prophecy, discerning of spirits, diverse tongues, interpretation of tongues, I Corinthians 12:7-11). See the #9 under Numbers.

VEIL=#7289, from #7286 in the sense of spreading; a veil (as expanded). This can be a covering, as in Heb. 10:20, "...through the veil, that is to say, his flesh." We must put aside our flesh (sin nature) in order to abide in His Presence.

VEIL OF THE FLESH represents the physical body created by God and houses His Spirit; the body is the temple of the Most High God. (Heb. 10:20; I

Cor. 3:16, 17) Hidden within the veil of flesh is the holy place (the soul), and the Holy of Holies (your spirit).

WALL in Hebrew has several types. A wall of protection is used in Exodus 14:22, 29, speaking of the escape from Egypt and the crossing of the River Jordan. In Gen. 49;22, "shur" is used and speaks of a wall of blessing. "Joseph is a fruitful bough, even a fruitful bough by a well; whose branches run over the wall (shur)." Then there are walls of separation, for good or evil. Leviticus 14:34, regarding the law of leprosy and refers to one of these walls. This is the type of wall used in this book. The meaning is "to trench, wall up, breakdown, cast out, destroy, dig" (#7023, from #6979). This type of wall isolates, separates and is used to make a home for idols.

WINDOW =(Strong's # 6672=tsohar, "a light (i.e. window); from #6671="to glisten; to press out oil: -make oil." from #3323="oil; anointing").

YESHUA – the Hebrew name of Jesus!

Resources for Deeper Study

EMDR: *Getting Past Your Past* by Francine Shapiro, PhD, Rodale Books.

HEALING: *Healing the Whole Man Handbook* by Joan Hunter; *Healing Starts Now!* by Joan Hunter; Destiny Image®Publishers, Inc.

LIBRARIES: Christian Classics Ethereal Library; ccel.org, for ancient books written by the early church saints. Saint John of the Cross

NUMBERS: *Numbers in Scripture* by E.W. Bullinger, Kregel Publications. I recommend *The Wisdom in the Hebrew Alphabet* by Rabbi Michael L. Munk, Mesorah Publications, Ltd.

WORD STUDIES: *Understanding Types, Shadows, and Names Vol. 2* by Kelly Varner, Destiny Image® Publishers, Inc.

Meet the Author

I AM DAWN LINDSAY, AN ORDAINED MINISTER OF the Christian faith. To know God is my greatest passion on a daily basis, and to assist others in their pursuit of healing and spiritual growth brings me great joy!

In my early years I set out on a venture to know the deep things of the Lord and learned most of what I know of Him through and because of my marriage. Not surprisingly, my favorite books are Hosea and Song of Solomon, which focus on the mystical marriage between the lovers of God and our Maker Himself.

Along the way an intimate relationship with God developed into a personal ministry through my church. I was ordained in 1995, appointed as an Elder and headed the Women's ministry. Later, I began holding prayer workshops with tea's, bi-monthly Bible studies and provided personal ministry to many men and women.

Currently, I am a member of the 4 Corners Alliance founded by Joan Hunter, ordained through Joan Hunter Ministries and God's Grace Church, through Pastor Al Dube. I am an author, speaker, workshop facilitator and personal spiritual coach.

Acknowledgements

Many Thanks To...

My Heavenly Father, Lover of my soul! I adore You! You are my all in all! Thank-you for making me and choosing me for Your own; for picking me up and cradling my shattered soul in Your everlasting love until healing manifested; and for authoring my everyday. I write for You and your Bride, for my tongue is like the pen of a skillful writer, whom You have created.

My earthly father, **Benjamin J. Taylor**, who, at the time of his graduation into heaven, gave me his Mont Blanc pen. He also passed on his DNA for writing. So it is that My Father's Pen © was created through both of my Father's! Thank-you, Daddy! I miss you!

Howard Lindsay, the love of my lifetime! We have been writing our book of life together since we were 19 years old. Without you, I would not be the woman I am today. Thank-you for all of the history we share, for without it, this book would have never been written. Aside from our Father, you have been my greatest teacher.

Howard C. Taylor, my brother whose love and respect held me in higher regard than I deserved. The life you lived here on earth is still teaching me. And I love you so much! You made the publishing of this book possible and I am so grateful!

My children, **Josh Ian Lindsay** (Computer Sciences Engineer) who once said prophetically that society was changing and a time would come when my skills would be appreciated (empathy, developer, positivity, relator, individualization-according to Gallop Clifton Strengths). You and your unique insights inspire me and always prompt a sense of wonder in those who listen. **Megan Shure-Lindsay** (daughter-in-love, Musician, Singer, Composer), you are every mother's dream for her son and your love and friendship to me is golden!

Kristin Lindsay-Kempff, (Counselor/Therapist for the voiceless in society) whose respectful accountability, spiritual and professional insights have kept me writing. Thanks to you and **Heath (Kempff**, son-in-love, Professional Photographer) for providing a place to write, away from home. Your collective support of my writing really made a difference in the way I valued my talent and myself.

Tasha Lindsay-Mehl, (Artist, Author, Founder/CEO Olive Leaf Tea Co, Phoenix, AZ), whose encouragement and belief in this book kept it on my desk and not tucked away in a filing cabinet! You are a strong woman and an overcoming daughter of God, whose life is continually revealing deeper depths of His mystical Presence.

Elliot Lindsay, Quinn Mehl, Ethan Lindsay, Jonah Mehl, Carter Lindsay, and Cedar Kempff, my six grandchildren. Oh, how I love you!

Pastor Al Dube (God's Grace Church, Tempe, AZ) who prophetically saw potential in me when there was no outward evidence of such; whose Biblical integrity taught me how to rightly divide the Word of God and to see deeper than superficial text, diving into the deeper levels of meaning in the Word.

Victoria Bjerke, my precious friend, (author of Little Weed; speaker; intercessor and prophetic warrior) whose constant, faithful friendship, encouragement and intercession literally saved my life.

Cindy Rodriquez (Prophetess, Marketing Queen and long-time close friend) who's prophetic prodding and anointed action-plans held me to the task **Pauline Sandell** (Global Age Life Coaching) whose editing and insights were priceless. These three women spoke life to me when I thought the book was worthy of the trashcan. All three of you performed the role of midwives in the final stage of birthing this book.

Adam Robinson (Good Book Developers; formatting, design, cover design) You have a way of mixing kindness into your professional expertise to help naive authors make decisions that will bring forth a beautiful and excellent product. Thank-you! You've been great to work with!

Walter Larsen (WalterLarsenImages.com, Cave Creek, AZ) You are a gifted photographer, making an ordinary person feel like a movie star! Thanks for making it fun!

Amanda Victoria, (Make-up Artist, Hair Specialist; Founder and CEO of Amanda Victoria Beauty, Bringing Beauty to the Desert, Phoenix, AZ), who's talent for bringing inner beauty to the visible realm made me shine in my photo-shoot. God's Spirit in her draws out the Living Waters in others. Thank-you for seeing "me!"

If the psychological building of a person's soul could be compared to an interior designer, **Soozie Bolte**, MC, LPC, LISAC, would be the inspector and accessorizer of my house! Thank-you for all you've done for me!

God leads me to the best people! You are all so very talented, gifted by God and have impacted my life in more ways than you know. I am blessed because of you and I am looking forward to spending eternity with you all!

Workshops

Feeling stuck? Need healing? Shattered from sexual abuse? Longing for a more intimate relationship with your Creator? These workshops are powerful times of personal revelation, healing and break-through from long-standing hindrances into personal victory, launching into your next season of soul prosperity.

> *"Beloved, concerning all things I wish that you may prosper and be in health, even as your soul prospers." 3 John 2*

(SCHOLARSHIPS MAY BE AVAILABLE BY SPECIAL REQUEST)

RE-MEMBERING

For those shattered souls, whose spirit is perhaps broken;

Have your life circumstances and choices eroded your hope for anything good?

Do you sense a profound "sleeping" within, living life but not living with a freedom to be?

Are your emotions numb, feeling that you are sleepwalking, living life but not really connected?

Is there trauma in your past?

Have you walked in the heavenly places, fallen from Grace but can't seem to return?

This workshop offers not only hope, but also methods for integration for the shattered places of your soul. It takes you through Dawn's book, *The Unicorn, the Donkey and Darling* with additional exercises and hands-on personal ministry.

FIND YOUR DANDELION LIFE!

If you are transitioning from something but don't know to what, this may be the workshop for you!

This is a small group workshop dedicated to a process, worked one-on-on, to excavate your deepest desires for your life, thus revealing the Lion's life in you. You will leave the workshop knowing:

- Your personal core values that drive your life
- What you personally must be faithful to in order to be happy
- Your unique call

- How to know when you are on your divinely inspired path

INTIMACY WITH GOD

To many, prayer is merely a one-way dialogue full of requests and frustration, But your relationship with God can be so much more fulfilling!

In this workshop you will find:
- How to hear God speaking to you.
- Biblical grounds that God has designed you to hear him
- How to develop your hearing ear
- How to distinguish God's voice from your own and others
- How to access the abiding presence of God available to you through "Listening Prayer"
- Resources to help deepen your relationship with God

"I want to know Him and the power of His resurrection and the fellowship of His sufferings, being conformed to His death." Phil. 3:10

MARRIAGE & GOD

- Learn how your marriage may reflect your relationship with God
- Learn the symbolism in the Hebrew wedding ceremony and how it all applies to you, married or single!
- Learn the warning signs of an affair, both spiritual and natural
- Learn how to recover from both types of unfaithfulness
- Learn why some marriages fail and others don't
- Learn about fairy tales and the truth about marriage
- Discover the beauty of Biblical jealousy in a marriage

Made in the USA
Columbia, SC
01 April 2022

58380028R00117